After the Storm

Ernest Hemingway's

After the Storm

The Story, plus
the Screenplay and
a Commentary by
A. E. Hotchner

CARROLL & GRAF PUBLISHERS, INC.
NEW YORK

First Carroll & Graf edition 2001

Carroll & Graf Publishers, Inc.
A Division of Avalon Publishing Group
19 West 21st Street
New York, NY 10010-6805

Library of Congress Cataloging-in-Publication Data is available.
ISBN: 0-7867-0837-9

Manufactured in the United States of America

In memory of my good friend
Jack Hemingway

Foreword

THERE IS PROBABLY no form of writing more perilous by nature than the adaptation: If the dramatic version succeeds, the author of the original novel or short story is hailed for indestructible genius; if it fails, the writer who adapted it is blasted for defaming the master. The adapter lives under the gun.

Over the years I have dramatized sixteen of Ernest Hemingway's works for the screen, including his only play, *The Fifth Column*, and his novel about the Spanish Civil War, *For Whom the Bell Tolls*. Most recently I have expanded his seven-page short story, "After the Storm," into a feature-length motion picture. Like most of his short stories, "After the Storm" delineates characters and a situation that require expansion in every direction. Therein lies the peril for the adapter.

Adaptation, by its very nature, forces playwrights to deal with people not their own, set against backgrounds not of their invention. With varying degrees of success the adapter tries to identify with these people but does not often succeed, for it is like adopting a full-grown orphan. Years ago, I dramatized the Hemingway short story "The Gambler, the Nun, and the Radio" for *Playhouse 90* and found that, try as I would, I could not get inside the Hemingway characters in that story. As a result, the show never generated the warmth and excitement that it should have. On the other hand, I was able to get deep into the hide of Philip Rawlings, the sardonic hero of *The Fifth Column*, so that the character, as played by Richard Burton, had all the complicated insides that I feel Hemingway intended him to have.

There are actually five varieties of adaptations—and by adaptation I mean the conversion into a movie of a work not written for that purpose. First, there is the Scissors Adaptation: take a classic play, use scissors and paste . . . voilà! . . . a screenplay. Examples: the offerings of W. Shakespeare, H. Ibsen, or G. B. Shaw.

Second, there is the Distilled Adaptation. This involves taking a large work, usually a novel, and boiling it down to a manageable length. The process is deceptively difficult, as I found out with *For Whom the Bell Tolls*, but on those rare occasions when it works it has profound results, as witness *Gone With the Wind*.

Third, there is the countering process, the Expanded Adaptation. Here the basic material is brief—a mood, a situation, a set of unresolved characters—and it is up to the adapter to fashion a screenplay that is bigger than the source from which it sprung. It can be categorically stated that this process contributes more disasters than all the others put together. I suspect that many critics keep certain key words on call for these efforts: "thin," "obviously padded," "watered down," and "dissipates the incisive effects of the original."

The fourth type of adaptation is that of Straight Conversion: The source material in length, scope, and characters is just right for the screen. From this process, generally speaking, come the most rewarding adaptations, but most of the stories in this category have been consumed. Hemingway's "Fifty Grand" is one of them.

The fifth adaptation variety I can only label as the Wild Adaptation. This process entails taking a basic work and converting it beyond its apparent resiliency, invariably with catastrophic results.

Such a catastrophe had occurred in connection with an adaptation of Hemingway's short story "Fifty Grand," as it was presented on the *Schlitz Playhouse*. The Schlitz people were pretty faithful to the original story, except for one mutation—they changed the ending so that it was exactly the opposite of the Hemingway story and killed its entire premise. This dramatization created quite an ugly stir. *The New York Times*, for instance, called it "literary butchery," and Hemingway called it a lot worse than that, instructing his lawyer to keep him off the tube forevermore.

But when the renowned producer Fred Coe, then producing *Playwrights '56*, asked for the rights to "The Battler," Hemingway agreed on the condition that I would adapt it. My first screenplay, it was a classic illustration of the Expanded Adaptation. If you timed the ten pages that comprise the story, you might, by reading slowly, consume twelve minutes. And yet, from a dramatist's point of view, there was something compelling in the part of the Battler, a battered hulk of a once-champion prizefighter whom Hemingway describes thus: "In the firelight . . . his face was misshapen. His nose was sunken, his eyes were slits, he had queer-shaped lips. . . . The man's face was queerly formed and mutilated. It was like putty in color. Dead looking in the firelight."

From what the story told me, from what I remembered of a punch-drunk fighter I had once known, and above all from what I knew about the style and thinking and attitudes of Hemingway, whom, by then, I had known for eight years, I had to create dramatic scenes that matched, motivated, and somehow enhanced the basic fragment. Luckily I had two splendid people to work with— Fred Coe to produce, Arthur Penn to direct—and, eventually, an excellent cast: James Dean as the Battler, Phyllis Kirk as the girl who once loved him and was his manager, and a young Broadway actor, Paul Newman, as Nick Adams, who is running away from home and meets up with the Battler at a trackside fire.

We prepared for rehearsals with high hopes, but a few days before we were to begin, Dean was killed in a tragic sports-car accident and we were without a star in a very exacting part. This was a live show, and the actor who portrayed the Battler was required to play him at various times during his life. There was little time to find a star to replace Dean, but Penn had worked with Newman at the Actors' Studio and decided to take a chance with him. Paul took a room in a downtown Los Angeles flophouse, sharing it with a punch-drunk bum. He studied the bum's speech and his walk and his manners, and although the smell Paul brought each morning from the flophouse to the rehearsal hall made inhalation a bit painful, the character he eventually portrayed was a triumph, helped immeasurably by Arthur Penn's meticulous direction. The day after the telecast, Warner's gave Paul the Rocky Graziano lead in *Somebody Up There Likes Me*, and he was off and running.

As I mentioned previously, the snare of adaptation for the playwright is dealing with someone else's people set against someone else's background. Thus, faced with the problem of carrying forward a plot only partially developed by the source writer, the playwright must, in addition to the usual demand of whether the development is valid in structural terms, also strive for the kind of development that the source writer would approve. When I carry forward a Hemingway situation, I must consider whether the movement and the people are in keeping with what Hemingway himself would have done, had he been doing the adaptation. I try to determine this, not just from the nature of the particular story I am adapting but from everything I know about all Hemingway has written. For each story, play, or book an author writes is a blood relative of all the others. Or, to paraphrase Mr. Donne, no story is an island, entire unto itself; every story is a piece of the continent, a part of the main. Yet I know producers and writers who attack (and I use that verb in its most violent sense) a literary classic as if it were surplus Judith Krantz. How can an adapter read up on Zola, Dickens, or Dumas when the producer must have a script in four weeks? And Meryl Streep won't sign for the lead until she sees a script. Anyway, look at it this way, kid: When you've seen one Picasso you've seen 'em all.

Complete knowledge of an author's work and biographical existence is not necessarily important for the specifics it contributes; the adapter, either by choice or contractual limitation, may not use actual characters or incidents from the other works, but their value for the adapter is in providing an undeniable richness of viewpoint.

To know the author personally, as I knew Hemingway, is even more helpful—but seldom is the original author available.

The adapter's chief nemesis, the tricky matter of keeping style, is much more difficult than following the structural line. Any change of style, even the slightest, can disrupt the entire drama. Yet imitation, which is an easy refuge, can also be an easy disaster, for parody is imitation's inevitable shadow. So the playwright is forced to perform a high-wire act: to write the invented scenes as if they were the adapter's own, while preserving the spirit of the basic material that motivated them; to beware of any invented character who could not conceivably have come from the gallery of people the author has written about.

To give you a practical illustration of the problem the adapter faces when expanding a subjective prose thought into a dramatic scene, here is a passage from "The Snows of Kilimanjaro," describing the futility that Harry, who is a writer facing death, feels about himself:

Now he would never write the things that he had saved to write until he knew enough to write them well. Well, he would not have to fail at trying to write them either. Maybe you could never write them, and that was why you put them off and delayed the starting. Well he would never know, now. . . . He had destroyed his talent by not using it, by betrayals of himself and what he believed in. . . .

There was so much to write. He had seen the world change; not just the events; although he had seen many of them and had watched the people, but he had seen the subtler change and he could remember how the people were at different times. He had been in it and he had watched it and it was his duty to write of it; but now he never would.

A dramatic and important insight into the dying Harry's mind—but how to dramatize it? In the teleplay I introduced a character, Harry's editor, Jim, whom he visits in a flashback. In addition to providing dramatic elaboration on the quoted Hemingway passage, the scene included other bits and pieces from the story, pulling them all together into the cohesive moment when Harry and Jim finally face a situation they had been avoiding for many years. Under John Frankenheimer's sensitive direction, Robert Ryan and James Gregory played this scene with just the right amount of anger, an anger rooted in the frustration both felt at their collaborative compromise.

EDITOR   It's a good theme, Harry. Of course it's hard to tell from three chapters, but I'd say it's provocative and ought to sell well.

HARRY   Is that the best you can say for it, Jim?

EDITOR   What do you mean, Harry? I'm delighted that you're back at the typewriter again after all this time. I suppose you have your new marriage to thank for that. Your talent has its own public, you know.

HARRY   What *is* my talent, Jim?

EDITOR   Oh, now, come on, Harry. You don't want a literary critique from me at this stage in our relations.

HARRY   Why not? Can you measure talent with a sales graph?

EDITOR   Now don't belittle the sales index, Harry—you just show me a great writer who doesn't sell. . . .

HARRY   I can also show you a lot of junkmen who are high on the best-seller list. What *is* my talent, Jim?

EDITOR   Oh, Harry. . . .

HARRY   Or was my talent—well, let me tell you—whatever it was, I've destroyed it. You know how? By not using it, by betraying myself and what I believed in, by drinking so much that I blunted the edge of my perceptions, by laziness, by sloth, and by snobbery, by pride, by prejudice, by hook and by crook. Here you are, Jim—a catalog of your old books. What was my talent anyway? Whatever it was, instead of using it, I traded on it. It was never what I had done, but always what I could do.

EDITOR   If you feel that way, then stop moaning over not using your talent and use it.

HARRY   As simple as that, is it, Jim?

EDITOR   This novel you've begun here—is it something that touches you?

HARRY   No, I guess not.

EDITOR   Well?

HARRY   Oh, Jim. . . .

EDITOR   Listen, Harry, as your editor, I'm perfectly content with the books you used to write. They're good books. I run a profit-making organization, and they sell well. But as your friend, I'm as disappointed in your talent as you are. You've always kidded yourself into thinking that you had to save the things that really Count—capital "C"—as if aging them was an end in itself, so the years pass and you write Literary Guild selections with your pencil held at arms' length—

HARRY   How else can you hold it?

EDITOR   —pretending to yourself that what you were writing wasn't really touching you because it didn't come from the private stock of experiences that you're hoarding. For what, Harry? What are you saving them for? For when?

HARRY   I've been saving them till I thought I knew enough to write them well.

EDITOR   That's also a convenient way not to fail at writing them, isn't it? Maybe you can't write them and that's why you keep putting them off. It's about time you faced yourself.

HARRY   Why face yourself? You turn all mirrors to the wall. I have good insides, so I don't go to pieces, and it's all in the attitude you take, anyway.

EDITOR   What attitude's that?

HARRY   I'll tell you, Jim, inside myself, I have a secret— that I will write about these people, about the very rich; that I am really not of them but a spy in their country.

EDITOR   So why don't you write it—this book about the
Very Rich you've been spying on? Why?

HARRY   Why? What is writing? Do I have to tell you, of
all people? Is it a whiff of oxygen after breakfast and
off you go—three thousand words before the lunch-
time martini? Don't sit here at your mocking desk in
this corporate tower and ask me why.

EDITOR   It happens to be my mocking job to ask you
why. Harry, why? It makes you mad to hear it,
doesn't it? All right, then, get mad. But hear it! I have
three chapters here that didn't come from your guts
or your heart or your head. You wrote 'em like a
coward.

HARRY   Shut up, Jim, you don't know what you're talking about.

EDITOR   You wrote 'em safe, like a coward! Deny it. Tell
me you didn't!

HARRY   I don't have to account to you.

EDITOR   That's right. You don't. And I'll put a stiff
cover on them and wrap a pretty jacket around them
and booksellers will put them in their windows and
no one, except you and me, will know, will we? I
don't matter, Harry—but how about you?

HARRY   *(after a long pause)* Tear it up.

EDITOR   Are you sure?

HARRY   Tear it up. *(Jim starts to tear the pages as the scene fades out.)*

I wrote a Hemingway-based stage play, *A Short Happy Life*—no relation to the story about Francis Macomber—containing a scene that is a variance of this same Kilimanjaro base. In the stage play, however, I interpreted the source material quite differently in terms of how Harry's frustration is expressed. I include it here to demonstrate the versatility of the spare ingredients Hemingway furnished in his short story.

MACWALSEY   Hello, Mr. Davis.

HARRY   Oh, hello, Professor. Please sit down. *(He pours a drink.)* Have a drink.

MACWALSEY   Thanks.

HARRY   *(obviously ill at ease)* I've been thinking—it was a hell of an imposition—

MACWALSEY   No, not at all. I enjoyed reading it very much. *(He takes a sheaf of manuscript papers from his pocket and puts them on the table.)* And I was flattered that you suggested it.

HARRY   But—I mean, I've just met you a couple of times here at the bar, and then to force my stuff on you.

MACWALSEY   It was a welcome relief from seventeenth-century French poetry.

HARRY   *(filling the glasses)* That your field?

MACWALSEY No, not exactly. It's just research I'm doing during my sabbatical. I'm mostly confined to
American literature.

HARRY Oh, I see.

MACWALSEY Eighteenth and nineteenth century. It's
pretty tough sledding when you go beyond Sam
Clemens. But let's not get into that or I'll be off
on one of my lectures. *(He picks up manuscript,
looks at it.)* I think you've got a good, provocative
theme here, don't you? Of course, eight chapters. It's
still not fully developed, but it should make lively
reading.

HARRY What about the characters?

MACWALSEY Well, of course, there's a lot of development. . . .

HARRY Sarah Manning. Does she command your in-
terest?

MACWALSEY Well, I think she needs some work. . . .

HARRY What do you find missing? If she doesn't work,
the book doesn't work.

MACWALSEY *(pours himself another drink; Harry re-
fuses offer)* She seemed a bit . . . well . . . contrived. I
didn't think she fell naturally on the page.

HARRY And her husband?

MACWALSEY There again, I'm sure you plan—

HARRY Listen, Professor, let me level with you. I've been several years without writing at all. Getting started on this book was murder. I kept postponing it and making excuses—you know how writers do. . . .

MACWALSEY And professors. . . .

HARRY So now that I've . . . what I mean is, it's not just another book by a guy who's been turning them out. But I can't kid myself about it. That's why I showed it to you. You're a pro and you don't know me, so you don't have to worry about my feelings. Now let's have it. I'm one of your students and this is my exam and you've got to put an honest grade on it.

MACWALSEY Well, it's highly readable and I'm sure it will do quite well on the best-seller list, but if you want me to compare it with your early books—

HARRY Yes, I do.

MACWALSEY I think the difference is that in writing those you were concerned with the people you were writing about; in writing this one you were concerned with yourself.

HARRY I guess that says it.

MACWALSEY But understand, I'm a teacher and my standards are different. . . . (Harry picks up the man-

uscript, tears it in half; MacWalsey grabs his wrist.)
Wait! You can't do that!

HARRY   Why not?

MACWALSEY   Because I'm . . . what do I know about publishing? Send it to your editor. Get his reaction.

HARRY   No. It wouldn't be honest enough.

MACWALSEY   Then get a publisher who's more reputable.

HARRY   He's very reputable. He wears a vest. He defers. But like all publishers he owns a hungry printing press. I'm tearing this up because what you say strikes home. This was written in a spirit of therapy. *(He tears the manuscript again, lets it drop.)*

MACWALSEY   My God, I had no idea—I feel terrible.

HARRY   So do I.

Hemingway's attitude toward my dramatizations was, from the adapter's point of view, ideal. He had a practical leniency toward the metamorphosing process, and his only concern was that the spirit and intent of his story and people were retained in the dramatized version. This is often not as easy as it sounds. For what you get from most Hemingway short stories are the people, the times, a nuance of the emotional problem involved; these ingredients are rich, but beyond them you are on your own. An Ernest Hemingway story is constructed, as he himself once described the process, like an iceberg, with a fraction above the surface and the bulk of it deep in the paper where it does not show. "The test of a good story," he once said, "is in how much good stuff you can leave out."

The spareness that results from this omission is the strength of his short stories, but in the process of converting them to dramatic form that very strength becomes a threat. Drama cannot be as elliptical as prose. And yet, if too much is filled in, the Gothic becomes baroque. The result is not iceberg but ice floe.

Although Hemingway never participated in the actual writing of my adaptations, he did like to see the finished product, and occasionally, although I am pretty fast on my feet, I was trapped into seeing one of my offerings with him. I do not know how other dramatizers react to watching their work in the company of the author whom they have adapted, but as for me, whoever estimated that a coward dies a thousand deaths was an arch-conservative. The time we saw the ninety-minute Part Two of *For Whom the Bell Tolls* is a good example. Hemingway and his wife and I were driving from Ketchum, Idaho, to Key West, Florida, and were scheduled to arrive in Phoenix, Arizona, the night of the telecast. Hemingway, who had not seen Part One because it had not been carried by Ketchum TV, was anxious to see this installment. It was his plan to check into a motel and see the play on the set in his room.

Ten minutes before airtime we checked into a primitive motel that had rabbit-eared television sets. Mary and Ernest made themselves comfortable while I fiddled with the dials, which in number anticipated the instrument board on a 747. About all I could achieve by twisting and pulling on the knobs was to change the direction of the blizzard that was permanently blowing across the screen. Two minutes before airtime we summoned the manager. He came equipped with a screwdriver and twisted something that eliminated the blizzard—but left the screen completely blank.

"Wal," he said, "the thing about these sets—they go back a piece, and about the only way you kin git a real clear picture is to grab ahold of one of them rabbit ears."

So that's how Hemingway saw *For Whom the Bell Tolls*—with me sitting next to the set aholding on to one of the antennae. Despite the adverse conditions, Hemingway liked the play very much, but he had one important criticism: He felt that by emphasizing Robert Jordan and his band of Loyalist guerrillas, I had not given sufficient balance to the Nationalists. In the novel, Hemingway had tried to be fair to both sides, and the bitter fight of brother against brother, joined as they are by a common background of heritage and faith, made a considerable contribution to the book's power. Specifically, what Hemingway missed in the television version was Sordo's defense of the hilltop that would have introduced Lieutenant Berrendo, a sympathetic character who represented the Loyalist point of view. The Sordo scene had been in my original script but budget limitations had necessitated its excision. "But, everything considered, the television play came out a damned sight better than the movie," Hemingway said. "That movie was Abercrombie and Fitch out of Helena Rubinstein." He telephoned Maria Schell the next day and told her what a fine performance she had given. "You really looked like you'd been in the hills for six months," he said.

WHEN DEALING WITH Hemingway material, censorship and criticism take on special significance. A prominent lady reviewer, writing her opinion of my adaptation of "The Killers" in a New York paper, said that it was "a fine, suspenseful melodrama" but that the innate limitations of TV kept it from being even better. "I have never read 'The Killers,' " the lady critic confided, "but I've read enough Hemingway to feel sure there was a great deal more to the story than was vouchsafed us last night." "The Killers" covers eleven pages in its published version, and I had used every bit of it in the adaptation.

The late John Lardner, a fistic and a Hemingway purist both, wrote a long review for *The New Yorker* of my adaptation of "Fifty Grand," approving most of the play but lambasting it nevertheless for having committed the pugilistic gaucherie of making the prizefighter, played by Ralph Meeker, a middleweight when the Hemingway story described him as a welterweight. When you consider that the welterweight upper limit is 147 and middleweight begins at 148 (which is Mr. Meeker's division), you can appreciate the reverence that Mr. Lardner had for both prize ring and Hemingway. Actually, one of the worst perils of adapting Hemingway or Faulkner, Thomas Wolfe or Dostoyevsky, is that the cultists of such writers have a reverence for their works that precludes any dramatic interpretation short of reading the original prose aloud. Their point is: Why should anyone want to see an approximation of the original masterpiece on stage or screen or television when all one has to do is open the book and get the genuine enjoyment of it? That is the classic argument against attempting adaptations: No matter how well done, they cannot on any level compete with the works that generated them. These cultists are absolutely right and there is no defense to their contention—except that the majority of the millions who saw *For Whom the Bell Tolls* and *Gone With the Wind* had not read the novels, nor did they ever intend to. However, any publisher or librarian will tell you that after such telecasts there is an enormous increase in the readership of the books adapted.

THERE IS A considerable difference in adapting a work for television as opposed to feature films. There are not the same constraints on how long you can film; where you can film; who, what, when, and how you can film—all of which affects what you write. No sense in writing a battle scene if the budget won't permit it. I was able to experience that difference when I worked with the same Hemingway stories on television that I later adapted to a film.

The movie was called *Adventures of a Young Man*. Its genesis was a series of stories Hemingway wrote about a Michigan boy named Nick Adams. Originally, for a new and ambitious CBS Sunday program called *The Seven Lively Arts*, I wrote a loosely organized dramatization of five of these stories under the title "The World of Nick Adams." There was something about that unspon-

:ored hour, subtly directed by Robert Mulligan and with a sensitive original score by Aaron Copland, that illuminated the boy, Nick, who is the hero of almost all the early Hemingway short stories. Hemingway did not see the program at the time of its telecast—he was living in Cuba—but months later, when he came to New York, we had a screening for him at CBS. "It's almost as close to the boy as I got in the stories themselves," he said.

Gratifying as that telecast was, I carried away from it a feeling that I had been constrained, and that the only way I could express a fully realized Nick Adams was in the larger and freer medium of the movie screen. I needed the vastness of the Hemingway country, the time to develop the rare and sometimes bizarre range of his complicated characters, and the freedom to let the material run to its natural length. So when Jerry Wald at Twentieth Century–Fox acquired the rights to the stories, I was pleased to sign on to write the screenplay.

I began work on the script, now changed to *Adventures of a Young Man*, the autumn before Hemingway's death; as with the television adaptations, I discussed with him the nature of the material involved and the general design of the screenplay. He was concerned that the stories might be considered autobiographical. "Nick Adams bears the same relation to my boyhood," he explained, "as Huck Finn to Mark Twain's boyhood." In other words, there is a strong resemblance, yet the art of interpretation interposed elements that had shaded fact to fiction. As it turned out, the movie uniquely highlighted the problems of dramatizing a "personal" writer. (Hemingway was once described as "a writer who lives it up to write it down.") I found maintaining the delicate line between fact and fictional interpretation an enormous challenge.

For this cinema version of Nick Adams I added five stories to the five used on television. All of these stories are about the eighteen-year-old Nick, who in the year 1916 broke away from his middle-class Middle West environment and set out to see what life was like beyond the barriers of home.

17

The stories are connected only by the fact that Nick appears in all of them; other than that, they are isolated experiences of fear, disillusionment, courage, love, war, and loneliness. Each one is a glistening shaft sticking in the heart of an emotional experience. But to fuse them and embellish them for the screen without disturbing their impact was a particularly difficult assignment.

Nick Adams and young Hemingway were rooted in the same soil, a small town of the northern Midwest: father a doctor; mother an overbearing clubwoman, a devotee of the musicale, and a disciple of the literal word of the Bible. How the lives of young Nick and young Ernest coincided, how they differed, what was the truth of fact and what was the truth of fiction, will forever be mysteriously interred in the four short stories on which the first part of the screenplay is based: "The Doctor and the Doctor's Wife," "Indian Camp," "The End of Something," and "The Three-Day Blow."

The same was true of the next sequence of events: In rebellion against the humdrum life of his home town, where he feared he'd be buried alive, Hemingway hit the road, as did his fictional counterpart. But what makes this rebellion so interesting is that it is not that of the cliché delinquent whom we have seen too often on television and movie screen, wearing a black leather jacket and cutting up old ladies with a switchblade; Nick is a law-abiding youth from a middle-class family, motivated by an internal gale that blows him from boyhood to manhood, striking out to see for himself what lies beyond the protected shores of his adolescent isolation. This emergence of the man in the boy, which Hemingway likens to the three-day blow sweeping in from the northern lakes, is the classic, universal, and fascinating phenomenon that lies at the heart of the Nick Adams stories.

"The Battler" and "A Pursuit Race" are the two stories that tell of Nick Adams's searing adventures as he heads east in pursuit of a goal more intuitive than intellectual. Although these two stories find their origins in Hemingway's experiences at a Chicago gymnasium, where he hung out for a while in hopes of becoming a professional fighter, they are, in substance, invented; but the emotional response of the boy to seeing, for the first time in his life, the extent to which men can be battered and maimed by their experiences was certainly autobiographical.

The third stage in the development of Nick Adams—his service in the ambulance corps of the Italian army—again bears striking similarity to Hemingway's enlistment in this service, and the stories involved—"A Very Short Story," "Now I Lay Me," "In Another Country," "A Way You'll Never Be"—have some of the strains that later emerged in *A Farewell to Arms*, but again the mysterious elements of interpretation often veer the printed page away from autobiography.

The concluding section of *Adventures of a Young Man* is concerned with Nick Adams's return to his hometown and a resolution, for him, of his way of life. This portion of the film, without benefit of a Hemingway story, had to be carried forward from the point at which Hemingway stopped.

In tackling this particular project, whose episodic nature made it more difficult to sustain than his stories and novels, which deal with the continuous development of one set of characters, I was painfully aware that Hemingway regarded all his previous movies, with the possible exception of *The Killers,* as disasters. *The Snows of Kilimanjaro* he derisively called "The Snows of Zanuck." I went to see *The Sun Also Rises* with him one afternoon, and he lasted seventeen minutes by my wristwatch. "You write a book that you like pretty good over the years," he observed, "and then you go in and see them do that to it, it's like pissing in your father's beer." He also said, "Any movie in which Errol Flynn is the best actor is its own worst enemy."

Considering the number of abortive attempts (in his estimation) that good writers and directors had made on such works as *A Farewell to Arms* (twice), *For Whom the Bell Tolls, To Have and Have Not* (three times), "The Short Happy Life of Francis Macomber," and "My Old Man," I approached the Nick Adams picturization in much the same frame of mind as, dressed as a matador, I had once approached the bull ring in Ciudad Real one hot afternoon.

I finished the first draft of the picture two weeks before Ernest died—in fact, on the day I went to Verona to join Martin Ritt, the director, and Jerry Wald, the producer, to find locations for the scenes that were to be shot there. I heard the bad news on the radio while waiting for a plane connection in the Madrid airport.

My plane was called and I picked up the briefcase in which I had the screenplay. Well, I thought, that's one more thing. He had hoped this would be a true movie, because he cared very much about Nick Adams. I had worked hard to stay as close to the boy as I possibly could, and make it work, but now he would never see it. . . .

As the jet took off for Milan, I recalled a fragment of my last telephone conversation with him. It was June 14; he was in the Mayo Clinic, I was in New York.

"How's the movie script going?" he asked.

"All right, I think. It's hard to tell."

"Well, Hotch," he said, "don't forget that old Cherokee saying— you pays your money and you takes your chances. Just don't play it safe. You haven't, have you?"

"No. I don't think so."

"Then you're all right. Even if it doesn't work, you're all right. The hell with playing it safe."

After the Storm

by

Ernest Hemingway

After the Storm

IT WASN'T ABOUT anything, something about making punch, and then we started fighting and I slipped and he had me down kneeling on my chest and choking me with both hands like he was trying to kill me and all the time I was trying to get the knife out of my pocket to cut him loose. Everybody was too drunk to pull him off me. He was choking me and hammering my head on the floor and I got the knife out and opened it up; and I cut the muscle right across his arm and he let go of me. He couldn't have held on if he wanted to. Then he rolled and hung onto that arm and started to cry and I said:

"What the hell you want to choke me for?"

I'd have killed him. I couldn't swallow for a week. He hurt my throat bad.

Well, I went out of there and there were plenty of them with him and some came out after me and I made a turn and was down by the docks and I met a fellow and he said somebody killed a man up the street. I said "Who killed him?" and he said "I don't know who killed him but he's dead all right," and it was dark and there was water standing in the street and no lights and windows broke and boats all up in the town and trees blown down and everything all blown and I got a skiff and went out and found my boat where I had her inside of Mango Key and she was all right only she was full of water. So I bailed her out and pumped her out and there was a moon but plenty of clouds and still plenty rough and I took it down along; and when it was daylight I was off Eastern Harbor.

Brother, that was some storm. I was the first boat out and you never saw water like that was. It was just as white as a lye barrel and coming from Eastern Harbor to Sou'west Key you couldn't recognize the shore. There was a big channel blown right out through the middle of the beach. Trees and all blown out and a channel cut through and all the water white as chalk and everything on it: branches and whole trees and dead birds, and all floating. Inside the keys were all the pelicans in the world and all kinds of birds flying. They must have gone inside there when they knew it was coming.

I lay at Sou'west Key a day and nobody came after me. I was the first boat out and I seen a spar floating and I knew there must be a wreck and I started out to look for her. I found her. She was a three-masted schooner and I could just see the stumps of her spars out of water. She was in too deep water and I didn't get anything off of her. So I went on looking for something else. I had the start on all of them and I knew I ought to get whatever there was. I went on down over the sand-bars from where I left that three-masted schooner and I didn't find anything and I went on a long way. I was way out toward the quicksands and I didn't find anything so I went on. Then when I was in sight of the Rebecca Light I saw all kinds of birds making over something and I headed over for them to see what it was and there was a cloud of birds all right.

I could see something looked like a spar up out of the water and when I got over close the birds all went up in the air and stayed all around me. The water was clear out there and there was a spar of some kind sticking out just above the water and when I come up close to it I saw it was all dark under water like a long shadow and I came right over it and there under water was a liner; just lying there all under water as big as the whole world. I drifted over her in the boat. She lay on her side and the stern was deep down. The port holes were all shut tight and I could see the glass shine in the water and the whole of her; the biggest boat I ever saw in my life laying there and I went along the whole length of her and then I went over and anchored and I had the skiff on the deck forward and I shoved it down into the water and sculled over with the birds all around me.

I had a water glass like we use sponging and my hand shook so I could hardly hold it. All the port holes were shut that you could see going along over her but way down below near the bottom something must have been open because there were pieces of things floating out all the time. You couldn't tell what they were. Just pieces. That's what the birds were after. You never saw so many birds. They were all around me; crazy yelling.

I could see everything sharp and clear. I could see her rounded over and she looked a mile long under the water. She was lying on a clear white bank of sand and the spar was a sort of foremast or some sort of tackle that slanted out of water the way she was laying on her side. Her bow wasn't very far under. I could stand on the letters of her name on her bow and my head was just out of water. But the nearest port hole was twelve feet down. I could just reach it with the grains pole and I tried to break it with that but I couldn't. The glass was too stout. So I sculled back to the boat and got a wrench and lashed it to the end of the grains pole and I couldn't break it. There I was looking down through the glass at that liner with everything in her and I was the first one to her and I couldn't get into her. She must have had five million dollars' worth in her.

It made me shaky to think how much she must have in her. Inside the port hole that was closest I could see something but I couldn't make it out through the water glass. I couldn't do any good with the grains pole and I took off my clothes and stood and took a couple of deep breaths and dove over off the stern with the wrench in my hand and swam down. I could hold on for a second to the edge of the port hole and I could see in and there was a woman inside with her hair floating all out. I could see her floating plain and I hit the glass twice with the wrench hard and I heard the noise clink in my ears but it wouldn't break and I had to come up.

I hung onto the dinghy and got my breath and then I climbed in and took a couple of breaths and dove again. I swam down and took hold of the edge of the port hole with my fingers and held it and hit the glass as hard as I could with the wrench. I could see the woman

25

floated in the water through the glass. Her hair was tied once close to her head and it floated all out in the water. I could see the rings on one of her hands. She was right up close to the port hole and I hit the glass twice and I didn't even crack it. When I came up I thought I wouldn't make it to the top before I'd have to breathe.

I went down once more and I cracked the glass, only cracked it, and when I came up my nose was bleeding and I stood on the bow of the liner with my bare feet on the letters of her name and my head just out and rested there and then I swam over to the skiff and pulled up into it and sat there waiting for my head to stop aching and looking down into the water glass, but I bled so I had to wash out the water glass. Then I lay back in the skiff and held my hand under my nose to stop it and I lay there with my head back looking up and there was a million birds above and all around.

When I quit bleeding I took another look through the glass and then I sculled over to the boat to try and find something heavier than the wrench but I couldn't find a thing; not even a sponge hook. I went back and the water was clearer all the time and you could see everything that floated out over that white bank of sand. I looked for sharks but there weren't any. You could have seen a shark a long way away. The water was so clear and the sand white. There was a grapple for an anchor on the skiff and I cut it off and went overboard and down with it. It carried me right down and past the port hole and I grabbed and couldn't hold anything and went on down and down, sliding along the curved side of her. I had to let go of the grapple. I heard it bump once and it seemed like a year before I came up through to the top of the water. The skiff was floated away with the tide and I swam over to her with my nose bleeding in the water while I swam and I was plenty glad there weren't sharks; but I was tired.

My head felt cracked open and I lay in the skiff and rested and then I sculled back. It was getting along in the afternoon. I went down once more with the wrench and it didn't do any good. That wrench was too light. It wasn't any good diving unless you had a big hammer or something heavy enough to do good. Then I lashed the wrench to the grains pole again and I watched through the water glass and pounded on the glass and hammered until the wrench came off and I saw it in the glass, clear and sharp, go sliding down along her and then off and down to the quicksand and go in. Then I couldn't do a thing. The wrench was gone and I'd lost the grapple so I sculled back to the boat. I was too tired to get the skiff aboard and the sun was pretty low. The birds were all pulling out and leaving her and I headed for Sou'west Key towing the skiff and the birds going on ahead of me and behind me. I was plenty tired.

That night it came on to blow and it blew for a week. You couldn't get out to her. They come out from town and told me the fellow I'd had to cut was all right except for his arm and I went back to town and they put me under five hundred-dollar bond. It came out all right because some of them, friends of mine, swore he was after me with an ax, but by the time we got back out to her the Greeks had blown her open and cleaned her out. They got the safe out with dynamite. Nobody ever knows how much they got. She carried gold and they got it all. They stripped her clean. I found her and I never got a nickel out of her.

It was a hell of a thing all right. They say she was just outside of Havana harbor when the hurricane hit and she couldn't get in or the owners wouldn't let the captain chance coming in; they say he wanted to try; so she had to go with it and in the dark they were running with it trying to go through the gulf between Rebecca and Tortugas when she struck on the quicksands. Maybe her rudder was carried away. Maybe they weren't even steering. But anyway they couldn't have known they were quicksands and when she struck the captain must have ordered them to open up the ballast tanks so she'd lay solid. But it was quicksand she'd hit and when they opened the tank she went in stern first and then over on her beam ends. There were four hundred and fifty passengers and the crew on board of her and they must all have been aboard of her when I found her. They must have opened the tanks as soon as she struck and the minute she settled on it the quicksands took her down. Then her boilers must have burst and that must have been what made those pieces that came out. It was funny there weren't any sharks though. There wasn't a fish. I could have seen them on that clear white sand.

Plenty of fish now though; jewfish, the biggest kind. The biggest part of her's under the sand now but they live inside of her; the biggest kind of jewfish. Some weigh three to four hundred pounds. Sometime we'll go out and get some. You can see the Rebecca Light from where she is. They've got a buoy on her now. She's right at the end of the quicksand right at the edge of the gulf. She only missed going through by about a hundred yards. In the dark in the storm they just missed it; raining the way it was they couldn't have seen the Rebecca. Then they're not used to that sort of thing. The captain of a liner isn't used to scudding that way. They have a course and they tell me they set some sort of a compass and it steers itself. They probably didn't know where they were when they ran with that blow but they come close to making it. Maybe they'd lost the rudder though. Anyway there wasn't another thing for them to hit till they'd get to Mexico once they were in that gulf. Must have been something though when they struck in that rain and wind and he told them to open her tanks. Nobody could have been on deck in that blow and rain. Everybody must have been below. They couldn't have lived on deck. There must have been some scenes inside all right because you know she settled fast. I saw that wrench go into the sand. The captain couldn't have known it was quicksand when she struck unless he knew these waters. He just knew it wasn't rock. He must have seen it all up in the bridge. He must have known what it was about when she settled. I wonder how fast she made it. I wonder if the mate was there with him. Do you think they stayed inside the bridge or do you think they took it outside? They never found any bodies. Not a one. Nobody floating. They float a long way with life belts too. They must have took it inside. Well, the Greeks got it all. Everything. They must have come fast all right. They picked her clean. First there was the birds, then me, then the Greeks, and even the birds got more out of her than I did.

The Adaptation

FOR THE ADAPTER, this is what there is to work with: a six-page soliloquy delivered by an unidentified boatman who tells about a dramatic, tragic event that took place in the Bahamas. With a fierce storm raging, the narrator has a fight, presumably in a barroom, knifes his assailant, and, to avoid capture, is forced to flee into a howling storm.

He manages to locate his boat and ride into the churning sea. Next morning, all is calm but wreckage is everywhere. The narrator discovers a lagoon where a large luxury yacht has sunk in quicksand, entombing all aboard. The narrator dives to the wreckage but, try as he might, he cannot break into the boat; in the end he has to abandon it.

To begin with, what is there about this brief story that motivated me to attempt the obviously difficult task of turning it into a full-fledged screenplay? Quite simply, I felt it touched something common to everyone, including myself: the desire for a windfall against great odds. The quest for sunken treasure has consumed man for centuries, along with an insatiable quest for sudden wealth as exemplified in multimillion-dollar lotteries, television quiz shows with huge payoffs, long shots at the racetrack, a twenty-dollar flea market painting that turns out to be a Cezanne, and so on.

Of the five types of adaptations I described, *After the Storm* falls into category three, the expanded adaptation. To achieve a viable screenplay, I would have to provide Hemingway's spare story with a beginning and a dramatic ending involving characters and action that would stay true to the basic story while injecting valid conflict. To do that, I had to answer a number of questions.

Who is the man who is telling the story—a beachcomber? a fisherman? an American? a Limey? Who was the man he fought with, an old enemy? What would have happened if he had, with help, succeeded in entering the wreck? What would he have found? The story mentions a safe with gold in it. If he had found it, how would he have opened it and what would he have done with the contents? Did he have a woman in his life? Two women? If he did collect the booty from the wreck, would there be someone who would try to muscle in on his take? Would he be apprehended for knifing the man he fought with? Would he escape with the loot or wind up empty-handed as he does in the Hemingway story?

All grist for the adapter's mill.

TRIMARK PICTURES

Presents

THE FOXBORO COMPANY, INC. PRODUCTION

BENJAMIN BRATT

ARMAND ASSANTE

A Film By GUY FERLAND

AFTER THE STORM

MILI AVITAL

SIMONE-ÉLISE GIRARD

STEPHEN LANG

NESTOR SERRANO

ARTHUR NASCARELLA

GUSTAVE JOHNSON

BARBARA ANDRES

BOB WALTON

Casting	REUBEN CANNON & ASSOCIATES
	And Kim Williams
Music By	BILL WANDEL
Costume Designer	LINDA FISHER
Production Designer	JAMES A. GELARDEN
Editor	CHARLES IRELAND
Director of Photography	GREGORY MIDDLETON
Co-Producer	KENNETH TEATON
Supervising Producer	MIKE ELLIOTT
Executive Producers	MARK AMIN
	PETER A. MARSHALL
Produced By	NELLE NUGENT
Based on the Story By	ERNEST HEMINGWAY
Screenplay By	A. E. HOTCHNER
Directed By	GUY FERLAND

Cast

in order of appearance

Arno	BENJAMIN BRATT
Coquina	MILI AVITAL
Grandmother Driscoll	BARBARA ANDRES
Thomas	STEVEN PETRARCA
Delivery Man	BERNARD GRAHAM
Janine	SIMONE-ÉLISE GIRARD
Woman at Bar	NANCY SINCLAIR
Mama Nima	ROSALIE STAINES
Willie	BOB WALTON
Jean-Pierre	ARMAND ASSANTE
Ortega	NESTOR SERRANO
Juanito	JAVIER CANOL
Dorothy	GRETEL
Father	DIRK MUELLER
Constable James Peters	STEPHEN LANG
Merimac	HUBERT FRAZIER
Second Youth	BRENT CRAWFORD
Third Youth	SEAN BEATON
Purser	JAKE ROBERTS
Louie Gavotte	ARTHUR NASCARELLA
Fat Lady	LYNN ANN LEVERIDGE
Card Player	EMORY KING
Mrs. Gavotte	JENNIFER BEALS
Orthwell	GUSTAV JOHNSON
Governor's Wife	JILL JACOBSON
Steel Heiress	LEIGH CHAPMAN

Ernest Hemingway's

After the Storm

Screenplay by

A. E. Hotchner

1 INT: FULL SCREEN—MAP
The main titles play over an old nautical map of the Bahamas, the stretch of cays (small islands) trickling away from the Florida Keys toward the Dominican Republic and Cuba.

DISSOLVE TO:

2 EXT: A BEACH—DAY
ARNO *is scavenging the deserted beach. He is in his thirties, tanned, wears old white ducks, sneakers, no top, a long-used nondescript hat.*

He finds nothing but flotsam and valueless junk. The surroundings are beautiful—palm trees, sun, wildlife—but Arno only inspects an old shell. He throws it aside and rummages through the debris. He finds a yachting cap, a weathered binocular case with binoculars intact, sunglasses with one lens missing, which he playfully plunks on his nose, then tosses away.

He finds a small anchor, a pair of tennis shoes tied together, a billiard cue; then, farther along, under some seaweed, he finds several articles of women's clothing: a bra, a wraparound skirt. He looks around, looks at the clothes, calls out to the bush:

ARNO   Hello? Anybody there?

No one. We hear Bahamian music, lively and thumping.

We cut to a buoy, bobbing up and down in placid turquoise water. The music continues.

3 EXT: BOAT BOW—SAME DAY
Arno is steering the boat toward the buoy. The name on the bow is CACA DE TORO. *The music is coming from an Atwater Kent radio of the thirties.*

The Caca is a rather beat-up twenty-footer with a canopy supported by four-by-fours, a type of boat that is peculiarly Bahamian. A makeshift Murphy bed is snugged against the ceiling of the canopy, held there by ropes that lower it to the deck on pulleys. A big mop is stuck in the aft starboard well, a well meant to contain a deep-sea fishing rod. The interior of the boat is very comfortable—a table, a rack with books, etc.—appurtenances that tell you Arno spends a lot of time aboard. A clothesline strung aft has some clothes on it. The Caca tows a little skiff. There is a pot boiling on the small cookstove.

Arno drifts up to the buoy and bends over the side of the boat. He catches the buoy, starts to pull up the very long rope attached, and finally brings a lobster trap to the surface. There is a lobster in it, which he removes. He tosses it into the boiling water. He pulls up another rope attached to the underside of the trap and hauls in a net that contains two bottles of beer. With an opener that hangs from a chain around his neck, he opens one of the bottles. Ah! The first bottle of the day. Wonderful!

Arno settles himself into a canvas deck chair and sips his beer as he awaits the cooking lobster. He pulls his hat down over his eyes.

RADIO ANNOUNCER *(voice-over)* At the gong, the time will be
    twelve o'clock noon.

(*as gong sounds*) This is the Bahamas Radio Network, Saturday, September ninth.

The radio plays a recording of Eddie Cantor singing "Now's The Time to Fall in Love."

The lobster-pot water continues to boil. Arno dozes for a minute under the sun.

A light wind touches a rope that hangs over a pulley. The rope touches the flame on the stove.

The wind grazes Arno's face, and he scratches his nose. He smells something.

The flame has crawled up the rope and is now devouring his canopy.

Arno opens his eyes.

ARNO   Oh, no!

He leaps up and grabs the lobster pot, dumping its contents on the fire. He burns his hands but saves his boat. Lunch is history.

4 EXT: DOCKS, PIRATE CAY—DAY
Arno, after securing his boat at a dock where a sign proclaims PIRATE CAY, *starts toward the sleepy town carrying the burnt canvas canopy. The year is 1933.*
MAIN TITLES END.

CUT TO:

5 INT: SAILMAKER'S SHOP—SAME DAY
On the wall is an old plaque:

DEAD-EYE DRISCOLL'S SAIL SHOP—EST. 1783

An old lady looks up from her sewing machine as Arno enters. It is a small, old, quaint shop with models of sails, bolts of sailcloth, sewing machines, etc., compacting the room. Two men sew sections of sail by hand. A customer is in the shop being waited on by a young, truly beautiful girl, COQUINA DRIS-COLL. The old lady at the sewing machine is her GRAND-MOTHER.

Arno carries the section of canvas up to the counter.

ARNO *(to the old lady)* Good morning, Mrs. Driscoll. Need another patch-up.

He unfurls the canvas. There has to be a hundred patches.

The Grandmother looks at the burn and shakes her head.

GRANDMOTHER You're trouble, Arno.

Coquina turns to face Arno, and he notices her for the first time.

COQUINA Hello, Arno.

Coquina speaks with a pronounced Irish brogue. In fact everyone on this cay speaks with this accent.

ARNO Coquina? Good God . . . look at you!

The Grandmother takes the canvas from him.

GRANDMOTHER That'll be six dollars up front.

ARNO (*to Coquina*) You disappeared . . . three years—?

COQUINA To my uncle's sail shop on Wishbone Cay.

GRANDMOTHER And grew up before she went further with the likes of you, ten years older, living by selling the junk you find on the beach.

ARNO A "rugged capitalist."

GRANDMOTHER There are plenty of hard-working young men here who . . .

ARNO (*to Coquina*) . . . would bore you to death.

Coquina smiles, studying him.

COQUINA How's Dorothy?

ARNO She asks about you all the time.

COQUINA And you?

ARNO I put fresh flowers around your picture every day.

GRANDMOTHER (*Trying to break it up*) Coquina, you've got to get to the chemist's before he closes.

COQUINA (*to Arno*) If I don't get her laudanum, she'll be up all night. Want to walk with me?

They start to leave.

GRANDMOTHER Six dollars, Arno—we don't take IOUs.

6 EXT: STREET—DAY

ARNO   Grandma Driscoll doesn't like me.

COQUINA   I'm afraid not.

ARNO   Why? A man of such charm, imagination, self-reliance. . . .

COQUINA   A good-for-nothing beachcomber.

Arno shrugs it off as a local man, THOMAS, *walks by them, young and handsome.*

THOMAS   Top of the day to you, Coquina!

COQUINA   Hello, Thomas.

THOMAS   Arno.

Arno nods.

COQUINA   How's the house coming along?

THOMAS   Fine and dandy. Roof's on.

*Thomas nods to a banner they stand under—*ANNUAL LOBSTER ROAST AND DANCE SEPT. 15—*strung across the road.*

THOMAS   (*cont'd*) Would you go with me?

COQUINA   Sure.

Thomas smiles and leaves, giving Arno a glance. Arno and Coquina continue on.

ARNO   Grandma's kind of guy. "A fine, upstanding shopkeeper who can take over the sail business."

COQUINA   (*laughing*) She's looking out for me *and* herself. I'm the only family she's got.

ARNO   So you stay here for Grandma's sake?

COQUINA   As far as I can tell, there's no place better.

ARNO   That's because you've never been anywhere else.

COQUINA   You have, and yet you stay.

Arno's caught.

COQUINA   (*cont'd*) Why?

ARNO   To avoid money, possessions, and predatory women.

They are at the chemist's. They stop at the door.

ARNO   (*cont'd*) But what if I should fall in love with you?

COQUINA   Oh, Arno. You hardly know me, or me you.

ARNO   I'm glad you're back—more than glad. See you again?

Coquina mulls it over.

COQUINA   It's up to you.

She enters the shop, and Arno continues on his way.

41

7 EXT: DOCKS—BIMINI ISLAND—DAY

Arno is aboard Caca. *He wears a top now, a striped boat-necked shirt that was popular in the thirties. The gold chain of his pocket watch is draped across the side of his pants.*

As Arno gets off his boat, a Bahamian DELIVERY MAN *approaches him, carrying a large carton that is filled with food and whiskey.*

MAN Excuse me, mister, this the *Neptune's Delight*?

The man is referring to Arno's boat.

ARNO Can't read?

MAN No, sir.

ARNO Yeah—this is it.

The man puts the carton on board and starts away. As Arno realizes that this poor barefooted man will be held accountable for the supplies, Arno's delight in the scam quickly fades. He sighs.

Arno picks up the box and places it on the Neptune's Delight, *berthed in the slip across from the* Caca.

8 EXT: MAIN STREET—ALICE TOWN (BIMINI)—DAY

Arno walks along the bustling main street with a rod and reel. The binoculars he found are draped around his neck. The display in front of a jewelry store catches his eye. There is a very attractive bracelet in the storefront window.

Arno studies the bracelet, then looks at his fishing rod and binoculars. . . .

9 INT: BEDROOM—A CHEAP HOTEL ROOM—LATE AFTERNOON

The bracelet is being slipped onto a woman's wrist. Arno is in bed with a lovely Frenchwoman, JANINE. They have just made steamy love: in the afterglow, Arno has given her his present. She is delighted with it. Holding her arm high, she turns it this way and that to catch the light. Then she rolls toward Arno and nuzzles him.

JANINE (*French accent*) You know something, Arno? You've got style.

ARNO How so?

JANINE You give me the present after, not before.

ARNO Maybe it's a memento.

JANINE All the better. Isn't it nice you have me for your love life?

Arno sighs.

ARNO You're not my love life, you're my sex life.

JANINE And your love life?

Arno shrugs enigmatically.

JANINE (*cont'd*) Maybe you should get it together.

ARNO You know, you're right. My sex life's gotta go.

She sits up.

JANINE What?

ARNO Let's end it pretty.

JANINE So it's good-bye, just like that?

ARNO You would do it to me, in time.

JANINE I was just something that washed up on the beach?

ARNO Yeah, a treasure from Jean-Pierre's boat and I'm re-
turning it.

Janine looks at him, trying not to be sad as she lights a cigarette.

JANINE Scavenger.

*Arno tries to let it slide. He's been called nothing but a scav-
enger three times in one day.*

10 INT: SILVER SLIPPER BAR—LATER
Arno descends stairs from the guest rooms and walks into the bar.

*This is the hot night spot of Bimini, crowded after dark, quiet
by day. The bar adjoins a large room where there are tables
and a bandstand. It's a native kind of place, clean, orderly, with
a flair. MAMA NIMA, the owner's trusted second-in-command
tending the bar, is a big, fat, smiling Bahamian. One WOMAN
(white, well-dressed, fortyish, not unattractive) sits at the bar,
ignores the dart players, listening to WILLIE, the skinny piano
player, who is doodling at the piano.*

WOMAN (*to Mama*) Do you get many tourists in here?

MAMA NIMA   Some—now, in September, widows and dee-
vorcees.

*The woman laughs at having been so easily identified. Arno
enters and goes toward the bar, passing Willie, the piano player.*

ARNO   Hiya, Willie, how're the notes falling?

Willie, waves, smiles, and keeps on playing.

MAMA NIMA   Hey, Arno, heard that pretty bird's flew back.

*Arno slides onto an empty stool at the bar, next to the woman.
He pays no attention to her but she can't keep her eyes off him.*

ARNO   Word travels pretty damn fast, don't it?

MAMA NIMA   Mama gets it faster than Western Union. Same
as always?

Arno nods. She starts to prepare two tequilas with lime and salt.

MAMA NIMA   *(cont'd)* Thank God I won't have to hear you
moanin' about that girl anymore. Three damn years of
moanin' all over Mama Nima's bar.

Willie sings "Something for Nothing."

ARNO   I got any mail, Mama?

MAMA NIMA   You got a bar bill.

*She reaches back to a row of pigeonholes with letters and small
packages in them, a sort of unofficial mail drop.*

ARNO   Can I have another coupla weeks, Mama?

Mama smiles.

Willie continues to sing his song. The woman tries not to look at Arno.

Mama gives Arno his drink and one for herself.

MAMA NIMA   On the house.

They click glasses and drink, go through the lime, salt, down-the-hatch ritual.

ARNO   I may still be moanin', Mama. They don't go for us pelicans on Pirate Cay.

MAMA NIMA   You'll handle 'em, Arno, just like you handle my bar bill.

Arno checks his pocket watch.

ARNO   Gotta go.

WOMAN   (*cutting in*) Nice watch.

ARNO   My old man's.

WOMAN   He had good taste.

ARNO   Yeah, good taste and bad luck.

He gets up and takes a handful of bar nuts, stuffing them into his pocket.

ARNO   (cont'd) (to Mama, indicating the Woman) Set one up—
on my tab.

Mama sighs.

WOMAN   What's it called?

ARNO   "Squeeze the lime, lick the salt, down the tequila, and
enjoy the day."

11 EXT: MAMA NIMA'S—DUSK
Arno exits.

12 EXT: DOCKS—DUSK
*Arno is heading past the docks, where there is a double-decked
charter boat.*

It is Jean-Pierre Lavalle's boat, larger than the Caca *and much
newer. It flies the* tricolore; *it has topside controls on an ele-
vated platform and outriggers for deep-sea fishing.*

*JEAN-PIERRE is a handsome, lean Frenchman, in his early forties,
who dresses impeccably. He charters the boat for a living.*

JEAN-PIERRE   Hey, Arno!

Arno stops, a little wary.

ARNO   Hello, Jean-Pierre.

JEAN-PIERRE   Come aboard, someone looking for you.

ARNO   Can't. Dorothy's home alone.

Arno stays put. A large, beefy Cuban named JOSÉ ORTEGA *emerges from belowdecks accompanied by a goon bodyguard named* JUANITO. *Ortega wears a white suit, white panama hat, two diamond rings, and a large diamond stickpin. He smokes a cigar.*

ORTEGA   Hey, Arno! I look for you! Big money!

Arno laughs.

ARNO   And big surprises like last time?

ORTEGA   Hey, amigo, we got you out of that, no? This time, guaranteed, no bad surprises.

ARNO   Doesn't Jean-Pierre do your errands?

Jean-Pierre sucks it in.

JEAN-PIERRE   I got a charter.

ARNO   Another rich bitch from Miami?

ORTEGA   You know the waters off Cuba better.

ARNO   Cuba? No, thank you!

ORTEGA   What's the matter you? You need money, this is five hundred bills up front.

He waves a wad of money at Arno.

ARNO   Money? Me? The man who's got everything?

ORTEGA Don't make me laugh. With me—you "get."

ARNO Yeah, what I get is my ass in a ringer like last time.

ORTEGA Arno, you listen me. I don't like anyone turn me down.

ARNO I don't like dirty money or dirty jobs, and as a matter of fact I'm not crazy about you.

Arno is on his way.

JUANITO I take care of him?

ORTEGA No. I need the son of a bitch. The *Caca*'s got a shallow draft, and Arno's the only one knows the waters around the Morro Castle. I find a way.

13 EXT: GUMALIMI CAY—EVENING

Arno is beaching his boat on Gumalimi Cay, which is his island. It is small and verdant, with a simple little shack on the rise above the shore. Arno built this place himself, and although it's rather crude he loves it and is happy in it. It has scant furnishings, but somehow the inside manages to be comfortable; in fact, rather cozy. There are fruit trees around the house. Especially noticeable is a large banana tree, heavy with fruit, and a grape tree laden with clusters. Beside the house is a catch basin, fed by two rain spouts from the roof, that stores rainwater.

ARNO (*approaching the house*) Hey, Dorothy, I'm home!

DOROTHY (*voice-over*) Hi, Sugar-pie . . . sugar-pie!

Arno goes in.

14 INT: ARNO'S HOUSE—CONTINUOUS
We see that Dorothy is an African Gray parrot, sitting on an open perch. Arno takes a bar nut from his pocket and offers it to her.

ARNO Brought you a cookie.

DOROTHY (*taking the nut*) Yum-yum.

There are books everywhere, and a hand-wound Victrola. Arno turns on the record that's on the turntable. An opera recording plays. The shack only has this one room, which has a snug kitchen at one end and an alcove at the other where Arno's bed is.

ARNO Dorothy, listen, I think I'm in love but the big question is—are you listening, Dorothy?—does she love me? Well, what do you think?

DOROTHY Give us a kiss, baby.

ARNO Thanks . . . you're a big help.

As Arno lies back in his bed, next to a burning oil lamp, he catches a glance of an old framed picture.

It is a picture of Arno dressed in a suit, younger, shaking hands with a distinguished-looking man, older than Arno. It is presumably Arno's father.

Arno stares at the picture.

15 BLACK-AND-WHITE FOOTAGE
As if the picture has come to life:

CLOSE-UP:

Arno's hand lets go of his father's.

DISSOLVE TO:

16   INT: ARNO'S HOUSE (COLOR)—CONTINUOUS
Arno blows out the flame on the gas lamp.

17   INT: CONSTABLE'S OFFICE—NIGHT
CONSTABLE JAMES PETERS is a tall wiry white man with a neat mustache and a two-gun holster. A burly deputy, MERIMAC, is with him. The door opens and Ortega walks in.

ORTEGA   Hey, Jim. I need that pelican Arno to sneak into the Morro Castle and get me three guys who don't have papers.

CONSTABLE   So?

ORTEGA   So Arno don't wanna do it. Nail him on something and get him to go.

CONSTABLE   And for my trouble?

ORTEGA   These guys are good pay. How about we split five thou?

CONSTABLE   Why not ten?

Ortega smiles.

ORTEGA   Why not? How you gonna do it?

CONSTABLE   I just might have a connection that could pay off for us.

18 INT: PIRATE CAY CHURCH—THE NEXT DAY (SUNDAY)
Coquina and her grandmother finish their prayers after service and exit with several other parishioners.

19 EXT: PIRATE CAY DOCKS—CONTINUOUS
Arno secures his boat; he then starts to leave the docks, but his path is blocked by three blond YOUTHS, *still dressed in their Sunday clothes. They are Pirate Cay natives; one of them is Thomas.*

Arno stops, makes no effort to push past them. They speak with the local accent.

THOMAS   Well, if it ain't Arno—getting to be quite a visitor!

SECOND YOUTH   How's the junk business, Arno?

THOMAS   Not junk, man—*treasure.* Some day he's going to find the Royal Ruby of Singapore.

SECOND YOUTH   Listen, Arno, tell us, on those deserted cays, you ever find a mermaid?

THIRD YOUTH   Hey, Arno—how do you "do it" with a mermaid?

THOMAS   Tell you what, Arno, why don't you go back on down to your boat and find yourself a mermaid?

ARNO   I'll tell you how to do it with a mermaid.

Approaches Thomas.

ARNO   (*cont'd*) I go right up to her—

52

He's very close to Thomas, now.

ARNO *(cont'd)* —and I say, Honey, what a beautiful flipper. . . .

He takes Thomas's hand.

ARNO *(cont'd)* I've never seen a prettier flipper than that.

And he flips Thomas over the railing into the water.

From across the way, Coquina has observed this and smiles.

20 EXT: GRAVEYARD—SAME DAY
Very old gravestone: DRISCOLL 1729–1797

Coquina and Arno are walking slowly along a line of Driscoll graves. Arno carries his repaired canopy. Coquina carries a bouquet of flowers. The names on the graves: Samuel Driscoll, Ann Driscoll, Mordecai Driscoll, James Driscoll, Harlan Driscoll, Darryl Driscoll, Esther Driscoll, Rebecca Driscoll. Coquina stops in front of the end tombstone: Rebecca Driscoll. She places her flowers on the grave and kneels in thought for a moment.

ARNO Why did a bloodthirsty pirate like Dead-Eye Driscoll settle down here anyway?

They leave the graveyard and start walking along the adjoining street.

COQUINA The woman who owned the sail shop tamed him.

ARNO Is the shop enough for you?

COQUINA   What do you mean?

ARNO   Well, what the hell's here?

COQUINA   A very nice life, that's what.

ARNO   Maybe, but there are places where there's more to life.

COQUINA   Like . . . ?

ARNO   Like Paris.

COQUINA   What would I do there?

ARNO   Oh, you could take carriage rides through the Bois de Boulogne when the chestnut trees are in flower; dine on oysters at Pruniers; walk the snowy streets of Montmartre; sleep in a downy bed at the Ritz and wake up to croissants and coffee in front of a cozy fireplace; shop in elegant boutiques on Saint-Honoré.

COQUINA   You've done all that?

ARNO   No, but I've seen enough of the world to know about it.

COQUINA   I thought you were happy here.

ARNO   Doing what? Diving for lobsters? Polishing shells?

COQUINA   But if you lived here, and worked here proper . . .

ARNO   I don't think the welcome mat will ever be out for me. Maybe it's time I moved on.

Coquina leaves the graves. Arno follows.

COQUINA My mother loved it here. My father hated it.

ARNO He ever coming back?

COQUINA I don't think so. I don't blame him for leaving. He wanted more out of life ... to travel and see things ... money. ...

Pause.

COQUINA (*cont'd*) His pirate blood, I guess.

ARNO Any in you?

COQUINA Maybe. ...

ARNO Let me see.

With that, he kisses her. They are a match. It becomes passionate.

ARNO (*cont'd*) Pirate blood, all right. ...

21 EXT: CACA—PIRATE CAY DOCKS—SUNSET
Arno returns to the Caca *with his repaired canopy. He motors away.*

22 EXT: CACA UNDER WAY—MOMENTS LATER
Around the bend awaits a luxurious private yacht. On its bow, in large letters: PRIDE OF CHICAGO.
The PURSER, *with a megaphone, calls down to Arno.*

PURSER Ahoy, there! Want to make a small run?

Arno looks up.

ARNO Depends. . . .

The Purser throws down a rope ladder.

PURSER It'll be worth it.

CUT TO:

23 EXT: DECK OF THE YACHT—MOMENTS LATER
Arno comes on deck and is met by the PURSER. *From the moment he steps aboard, the camera should concentrate on making us aware of the opulence of the vessel and the people on it; in fact, the over-opulence, for these are nouveaux riches. Everything about the yacht—its interior decor, the dress of the people—should bespeak 1933 money.*

PURSER Mr. Gavotte wants to see you.

They walk.

ARNO *Louie* Gavotte?

PURSER Yes, sir.

ARNO The *Pride of Chicago*, all right.

They pass shuffleboard players, ladies in deck chairs, a small bar with people sitting around it.

A very tipsy plump woman, overdressed, expensive jewelry, intercepts the Purser.

FAT LADY Malcolm, I need some of my big stuff for tonight's bash. Is Mrs. Ofanski wearing her diamonds?

PURSER   Yes, madam.

FAT LADY   Then I'll do my emeralds.

PURSER   Yes, madam. In a moment, madam.

FAT LADY   (*to Arno*) Who are you?

ARNO   The spirit of Christmas past, madam.

The Purser leads Arno to the afterdeck where a gin rummy game is in progress. Louie Gavotte, a short, tough man in the mold of Edward G. Robinson, is playing high-stakes rummy. Standing in back of his chair, leaning over him, with her chin on top of his head and her hands inside his shirt, is a luscious big-titted blonde.

GAVOTTE   (*without looking up*) You goin' Bimini?

ARNO   Yeah.

GAVOTTE   (*handing him an envelope*) Guy there, Roy Malone, Barclay's Bank. Give him this, tell him, "Louie leaves for Jamaica tomorrow and wants the stuff. Louie pays on delivery." Got that?

ARNO   Yeah.

GAVOTTE   Write it down for him, Malcolm.

ARNO   I said I got it.

GAVOTTE   (*giving Arno a long look*) You better have.

He picks up a couple of bills from the pile in front of him and hands them to Arno.

GAVOTTE *(cont'd)* Knock with two.

Purser and Arno walk away from the gin rummy table.

PLAYER *(voice-over)* Jesus, Louie, have a heart.

PURSER One other thing—Mrs. Gavotte has something—

ARNO That wasn't Mrs. Gavotte draped over Mr. Gavotte?

PURSER *(a slight smile)* No, sir.

24 INT: HALLWAY, *PRIDE OF CHICAGO*—MOMENTS LATER
Purser knocks.

MRS. GAVOTTE *(offstage)* Yes?

PURSER Purser, madam.

MRS. GAVOTTE Come in.

25 INT: MRS. GAVOTTE'S CABIN—CONTINUOUS

PURSER Here's someone who will make the run, madam.

It is an elaborate stateroom, but the blinds are drawn and it is dimly lit. Linda Gavotte does not look like she belongs to Louis Gavotte. She is thin, not unattractive, rather frail, young, with a birdlike quality about her. She sits at a desk, writing. Incongruous that she is married to Louie Gavotte.

MRS. GAVOTTE   You're going to Bimini?

ARNO   Yes, ma'am.

MRS. GAVOTTE   Could you please bring something from there?

She finishes addressing an envelope, seals it, and hands it to Arno.

MRS. GAVOTTE   (*cont'd*) It's a packet . . . a medication . . . I have pain. . . .

ARNO   When do you need it?

MRS. GAVOTTE   Tonight.

Addressing the Purser.

MRS. GAVOTTE   (*cont'd*) Where will we be, Malcolm?

PURSER   Off Morgan Cay I think, madam.

MRS. GAVOTTE   It's quite lively here at night. Champagne and music—the chef is from the *Liberté*—join us.

ARNO   Thanks, but I don't think I have the wardrobe.

MRS. GAVOTTE   *Please.*

Pause.

He looks at her closely. The pallor of her face, the nervous eyes. She shrinks a little from his inspection.

ARNO Okay.

MRS. GAVOTTE (*anxiously*) Just call that number. You will bring my packet?

ARNO If I say I'll bring it, I'll bring it.

MRS. GAVOTTE (*relieved, smiles at him*) Sorry—I'm just so unused to people keeping their word.

Arno takes the envelope and starts to leave.

As Arno leaves, the Purser goes to the ship's bridge.

26 INT: BRIDGE OF THE YACHT—STILL SUNSET
The Purser goes to the ship's phone. He makes a call.

PURSER Hello, Malcolm here. Mrs. Gavotte just gave the envelope to a pelican named Arno.

27 INT: CONSTABLE'S OFFICE—SAME
The Constable is hanging up the phone.

CONSTABLE (*to his deputy*) Keep an eye on Arno. You know what to do.

Merimac nods.

28 EXT: OMINOUS SECTION OF ALICE TOWN, BIMINI—NIGHT
A storm is kicking up.

Arno makes his way along a dark street. Merimac is tailing him, unseen by Arno.

Parked at the curb on a side street is an old beat-up van. There are two men inside. Arno knocks on the window. It rolls down.

ARNO   I've come for Mrs. Gavotte's package.

Arno hands the man the envelope Linda gave him. A distinctive package is passed back to him.

29   EXT: PARKED VAN—NIGHT
Arno leaves the van and goes out into the night. The van drives off.

At night, the shanty town is deserted, ominous. Arno looks up into the sky. No stars. Wind.

Rain begins to fall lightly on his face. He picks up the pace. Lightning flashes as he looks behind him. Is he being followed?

Thunder rumbles. Arno stops. Merimac, holding a gun, reveals himself.

MERIMAC   What would a nice pelican like you be doing in this neighborhood?

Arno is silent.

MERIMAC   (*cont'd*) Give me that package.

ARNO   It's for a sick woman.

MERIMAC   Give it to me.

Arno hands it over.

ORTHWELL   (*voice-over*) Now you give it to me.

As Merimac turns, ORTHWELL fells him in one blow. The huge Bahamian has materialized suddenly.

ARNO   Damn, I'm glad to see you, Orthwell!

ORTHWELL   Nasty part of town for a man to be alone.

They embrace.

Orthwell returns the package to Arno.

ORTHWELL   (*cont'd*) Next time you comin' in my territory, let me know.

ARNO   Word was the army killed you.

ORTHWELL   My friends gave me a very nice funeral. The army stopped lookin'.

ARNO   How's it going?

ORTHWELL   Oh, they do us, we do them.

Orthwell takes Merimac's gun.

ARNO   Where can I find you these days?

ORTHWELL   Papa Ray's joint on the beach. . . . This guy belong to Constable Jim?

ARNO   Yeah. Deputy.

ORTHWELL   Good ol' Jim. Always keep him in front of you. He do enjoy shootin' people in the back.

ARNO   Yeah, maybe I'm being lined up for target practice.

A palm branch blows past Arno's feet.

ORTHWELL   We better get under cover.

They separate and go off in opposite directions.

30   INT: SILVER SLIPPER BAR—CONTINUOUS
Arno enters, soaked to the bone. He tries to catch his breath and calm down.

The place is crowded and bubbling with "hurricane animation," a phenomenon that occurs whenever there is a super-big blow. Everyone assembles to ride out the storm together—the old "safety in numbers" philosophy. The small band plays lustily. Willie is the pianist. There are some British sailors dancing with a mixture of white and Bahamian girls.

All throughout the scene, Willie is playing and singing "Don't Let It Get You," which has a refrain the group joins in on.

From across the way, Jean-Pierre sees Arno and squints his eyes as he finishes his cigarette.

Ortega sits with his henchmen, turns, and notices Arno as he enters. Janine, who sits with Jean-Pierre, sees the look in Jean-Pierre's eyes.

JANINE   I think the governor's wife wants to dance with you.

Jean-Pierre is distracted from Arno and follows Janine's gaze to a couple at another table. The man is the distinguished-looking governor of Bimini, thirty years older than his young wife.

JEAN-PIERRE   You're probably right.

JANINE   Tell me, darling, do you ever get tired of the chase—
one conquest after another, ho-hum?

Jean-Pierre looks back to Arno.

JEAN-PIERRE   And you, my sweet?

JANINE   What about me?

JEAN-PIERRE   That bracelet on your wrist? I don't recall seeing
it before.

JANINE   Ladies like to receive presents—not that you would
know.

JEAN-PIERRE   The ladies get *me*. That's more than enough.

He leaves to dance with the governor's wife.

*José Ortega sits at a rear table with his bodyguard, Juanito.
Ortega sends Juanito to get Arno. Mama Nima watches Arno.*

*Jean-Pierre is now dancing with the governor's young wife, oc-
casionally glancing at Ortega. Janine sits alone at the table, but
her eyes are on Arno, not Jean-Pierre.*

*Arno sits down at Ortega's table, and Ortega pours Arno a
drink.*

ORTEGA   I been thinking it over. Two thousand. One thousand
now, one thousand when you come back.

ARNO   It's still no.

ORTEGA   What's the matter? You no like money?

ARNO   I like money—but I don't like *your* money.

Arno downs his drink, gets up.

ARNO   (*cont'd*) Besides, this storm will wash up a fortune. Thanks for the drink.

Arno leaves him. Ortega looks across the room and notes the Constable sitting at a table in the shadows. He watches Arno sit back at his place at the bar, then looks at Jean-Pierre.

ANOTHER ANGLE:

Jean-Pierre, dancing with the governor's wife.

WIFE   Is he watching us?

Jean-Pierre looks over her shoulder.

JEAN-PIERRE   No.

WIFE   He leaves again next Friday for a governors' conference.

JEAN-PIERRE   (*mouth close to her ear*) If I kiss the ear of the governor's wife, will she scream?

WIFE   Yes! Oh, Jean-Pierre!

A cascade of water suddenly breaks through when two doors blow open onto the dance floor. Two men rush to the doors to latch them.

The dancers continue, dancing around the puddle.

The lights suddenly go out, plunging the Silver Slipper into darkness.

JEAN-PIERRE (*to the governor's wife*) Now, don't scream.

He kisses her ear. She screams.

Matches are struck to light the candles on the tables and the kerosene lamps on the walls.

Janine goes to Arno, asks him to dance. They dance.

ARNO (*to Mama*) Keep an eye on this, will you?

Mama takes the package and puts it on the back bar. The Constable notes this.

Ortega arrives at the Constable's table and sits.

ORTEGA He still won't go.

CONSTABLE Yes, he will.

Constable nods toward the package on the rear bar.

While Arno and Janine dance, Willie, at the piano, is singing.

ARNO (*indicating Jean-Pierre*) Is that his latest?

JANINE Yes.

ARNO What happened to Mrs. Richbucks from New York?

JANINE   Oh, she's next week's charter. Four days. Just the two of them. Maybe I'll invite you to dinner. I make a wicked coq au vin.

ARNO   That's nice of you, but you seem to have forgotten our tender farewell.

JANINE   You know, Arno, you're not very good for a lady's ego.

There is a crash at the side of the room—the storm has blown a tree limb through a window. This stirs everyone up, the men rushing in from the bar to see what has happened. They push the limb back outside, begin to board up the window.

The Constable is at the bar where Arno left his package. He brings it over to Ortega, who slits it open. Arno and Janine continue to dance.

Ortega walks up to Arno. He is holding the package. They are standing at the rear of the crowd, which is concentrating on the tree limb. The goon Juanito is with Ortega. What follows is not noticed by the crowd until the very end.

ORTEGA   You left something at the bar, Arno.

Arno sees the package Ortega is holding.

ARNO   Hand it over.

ORTEGA   When you come back from Cuba.

ARNO   It's medicine for a sick lady.

ORTEGA   Take a look. . . .

Ortega holds out his hand; it has white powder on it.

ORTEGA *(cont'd)* Looks like heroin, tastes like heroin, smells like heroin.

Arno is at a loss.

ORETGA *(cont'd)* You no go, I hand it over, all right—to Constable Peters over there. Okay—what you have? A lotta jail or a little boat trip?

Arno grabs for Ortega's arm, gets the package. Ortega produces a switchblade knife, points it at Arno.

Ortega jabs the knife at Arno, who, faster, grabs Ortega's wrist and twists the knife up in the air. Juanito rushes to help. Janine cowers as an intense fight begins. Juanito grabs Arno's arm but in pulling it forces the knife forward, and it cuts into Ortega.

Ortega drops back, grabbing at his wound. A woman at the rear of the crowd observes this, screams.

The people in the crowd turn to see what's happening. Ortega has fallen to the floor, blood all over his white suit.

Arno stands over him with the knife in one hand, the package in the other. Jean-Pierre watches, horrified.

WOMAN *(shrieking)* He's dead!

Ortega's goon has gone to his assistance. The people in the crowd are moving toward Arno, who drops the knife, not quite realizing what has happened.

Arno runs with the package past Jean-Pierre, as the Constable and his men rush him.

CONSTABLE Stop him!

His deputies and Ortega's bodyguard start after Arno. Arno darts across the floor and out the door, the men in pursuit.

31 EXT: DOCK—MOMENTS LATER
Arno's skiff is pitching and bobbing in the turbulent water. Arno, breathless, dashes into the scene, jumps aboard, starts the motor, and takes off as the pursuing men arrive.

They fire shots at the departing boat, which is swallowed by the storm.

FADE OUT:

FADE IN:

32 EXT: CACA—FOLLOWING MORNING
The storm has passed. All is calm. The Caca is at a shore, among mangroves. Debris from the storm floats in the water. Arno wakes and surveys the scene. He is thoroughly lost and disoriented.

33 EXT: CHAIN OF SAND BARS—MORNING
Arno is under way. He passes a chain of sand bars and steers between and around them but sees nothing.

CUT TO:

34 EXT: COVE ENTRANCE—MORNING
There are several massive rocks on the outside of the cove mouth. The splintered remains of a boat is on one of the rocks. Arno goes into the cove, beaching the Caca.

Arno stands aft, surveying the vicinity. He arrests his sweeping scrutiny, holds on something that attracts his attention.

35 ARNO'S POINT OF VIEW
A large concentration of birds is making over something in a nearby lagoon.

36 EXT: SKIFF—MORNING
Arno is in his skiff, approaching the lagoon and the birds.

He cuts his engine, gets out his glass-bottomed bucket, and starts to inspect below. Makes a sudden, startling discovery. Puts his head close to the bucket's glass to get a better look.

37 ARNO'S POV—THROUGH GLASS
The bow of a ship and, on the bow, clearly: PRIDE OF CHICAGO.

38 BACK TO SCENE—UNDERWATER
Arno, having stripped off his clothes, dives down to the yacht.

The bow is not very deep, but the ship is on a sharp downward slant so that Arno must go abruptly deeper as he moves along the hull.

39 EXT: UNDERWATER/ABOVE WATER—VARIOUS SHOTS
He comes to the first porthole. Terrible shock as he comes face-to-face with the drowned fat lady who wanted her emeralds. She wears the same clothes but is bedecked with the emeralds. Her face, hair floating, is right up against the porthole window, a few inches from Arno's face. He recoils and quickly surfaces.

40 EXT: SKIFF AGAIN—MORNING
Arno sits pensively in the sun, thinking hard. Salt water drips off his chin.

His small boat bobs in the expanse of coast. With not a soul about, it is as it he is the only man in the world.

Arno breathes deeply. He'll be wanted for drug-running, for murder! How'd he ever get here? What did he do?

What is he going to do?

Arno looks back at the water surface, glistening like gold in the morning light.

He has an idea.

41 EXT: ABOARD CACA—MORNING
Arno picks up a wrench from his old toolbox and gets back in his skiff.

42 EXT: UNDERWATER—MORNING
He revisits the porthole with the fat lady. One of her hands, the fingers covered with emeralds, is right up against the glass. Arno reacts to this—all those emeralds just an inch or two away; he hits the glass as hard as he can with the wrench, but it doesn't even crack.

In the interior of the boat, he sees several people floating, their jewelry glistening in the water. All those in the salon were in evening dress when disaster overtook them. Arno hits the port-hole several times more, as hard as he can. It cracks but does not break or loosen.

Arno's nose is bleeding. As he ascends he passes a porthole, stops, recoils at what he sees.

It is Mrs. Gavotte, her face against the glass, her hair floating and eddying around her face. Gripped by a sudden anger, Arno smashes at the window with the side of his fist. He is frustrated and angry, but feeling sorrow and compassion, he spontaneously reaches out his hand and touches the glass, as if he could actually touch Linda Gavotte. Then, abruptly, he kicks off from the side of the boat and starts his ascent.

43 EXT: SURFACE—MORNING
Arno pops to the surface, gasping for air, blood streaming from his nose. He can barely swim the short distance to the skiff. He fights to get the air back into his starved lungs, is barely able to hoist himself into the boat.

In the boat, Arno, his head feeling cracked open, picks up a boat rag and holds it against his bleeding nose.

He picks up the package Ortega framed him with. Slowly, thoughtfully, he opens it, leans over the side of the boat, and gently sprinkles the contents over the surface of the water.

44 EXT: PIRATE CAY LOBSTER ROAST AND DANCE— NIGHT
There is a three-piece local band playing for the dancing, and tables are laden with food and drink. The area is illuminated by lanterns.

Lobsters are roasting on an open hearth. Coquina is a member of the party on the dance floor, Thomas at her side.

THOMAS   You know, the house I'm building, my father says it can be mine.

COQUINA   That's nice.

THOMAS   When I take a wife.

72

Coquina doesn't want to hear this.

COQUINA   I'm hungry.

She hurries off to get lobster.

ANOTHER ANGLE:

Using the cover of a copse of trees and shrubs, Arno is watching Coquina.

45   EXT: DANCE—LATER
Coquina stands sullenly over one of the tables, putting food on a plate.

Arno circles around to the table where Coquina is filling her plate, as Thomas drinks with his pals.

Coquina is putting a hot roasted lobster on her plate. As she turns away from the table, Arno pulls her into the thicket.

Coquina starts to protest, then discovers that it's Arno. He cautions her, with gestures, to be quiet.

ARNO   I need your help.

COQUINA   But why are you—?

ARNO   I'll explain everything, but right now you've got to help me.

COQUINA   Do what?

ARNO   Get some things.

COQUINA What?

ARNO Sledge hammer, crowbar, diving suit, air pump—

COQUINA What? Why?

ARNO I'll tell you later. It's important, really important. You must help me, Coquina. And I don't have much time.

Arno takes the plate from her.

ARNO *(cont'd)* I'm starving.

He starts to eat ravenously. She watches him.

Back at the lobster roast, Thomas realizes Coquina is missing.

46 EXT: GENERAL STORE—LATER
An old weathered building, with one door that says IN, *another that says* OUT. *The store is dark. Arno and Coquina approach the entrance, staying in the shadows.*

COQUINA *(whispering)* This is the Richardsons' store! Arno, it's wrong. You'll be arrested!

ARNO We'll bring the stuff back.

CLOSER SHOT—TWO OF THEM

Passing the rear of the store. Coquina pantomimes Arno to be quiet, points to the rear of the store to let him know the owner lives there.

AT THE "IN" DOOR—ARNO

He slits the screen with his pocketknife, reaches his hand in, opens the door.

47 INT: GENERAL STORE—MOMENTS LATER
The store is jam-packed with items of every description. A cat suddenly darts across the aisle in front of them, giving them a start.

Arno goes to the shelf and takes down a small sledge hammer

ANOTHER ANGLE

as Coquina leads Arno to another part of the store and points up to where the crowbars are.

Arno takes a ladder that is leaning against the wall and moves it to the crowbar shelf.

CUT TO:

48 EXT: GENERAL STORE—MOMENTS LATER
Thomas approaches the store, and takes out his key. Surprised to find the door open, he enters cautiously.

49 INT: GENERAL STORE—CONTINUOUS
Arno is mounting the ladder, reaching for a crowbar.

THOMAS   Anybody in here? Dad, you there?

Arno motions to Coquina to hide; then he climbs to the top of the ladder, puts himself out of sight. Thomas is coming down the aisle with a flashlight, shining it from side to side.

THOMAS   (*cont'd*) Who's here? Anybody here?

Thinking it's better to reveal herself than to be discovered, Coquina steps in his path.

COQUINA   Oh, Thomas, I wondered where you had gone.

THOMAS   Coquina! Gone? I didn't go anywhere. I was looking for you.

COQUINA   Well . . . well, I thought you had left and that it might be nice for us to be alone.

THOMAS   Really? Oh, sure, yeah . . . people around . . . you've been with that Arno fellow so much. . . .

COQUINA   Thomas . . .

He pulls her down beside him on a large coil of hemp rope.

THOMAS   I thought maybe you didn't care for me. . . .

He puts his arms around her, pulls her against him.

THOMAS   (*cont'd*) . . . the way I care about you.

He forces a kiss on her as she struggles away from him.

COQUINA   No, Thomas, listen, let me tell you—

THOMAS   Nice and cozy here. We might have us a little bang like you've been having with Arno. . . . C'mon, nice little bang—

He's trying to get at her; she's struggling.

Arno is directly above them. He has a bucket by the handle, centers it over Thomas's head, drops it.

ARNO   Bang!

The bucket hits Thomas square on the head, knocking him out.

COQUINA   Arno!

Arno swings down from the rafters.

He helps Coquina up.

ARNO   He'll be all right. Hurry!

Arno's light illuminates an old diving suit that is hanging on a wall peg, with a hard hat attached. Beside it is a rusty hand-operated air-pumping apparatus.

Pay dirt!

50   EXT: BIMINI DOCKS, JEAN-PIERRE'S BOAT—NIGHT

RADIO ANNOUNCER   (*voice-over*) We interrupt this broadcast with a bulletin. . . .

Jean-Pierre and Janine are on deck listening to the radio.

RADIO ANNOUNCER   (*cont'd*) The Fidelity Insurance Company has begun to search for *The Pride of Chicago*. Fidelity has a ten-million-dollar policy on the boat and its contents, a million dollars in gold. . . .

The broadcast continues; Jean-Pierre makes himself a drink.

JANINE   If you found the gold on that ship you wouldn't have to make love with all those charter ladies.

Jean-Pierre turns off the radio.

JEAN-PIERRE   I don't make love with them. I make business sex with them. With you I make love.

JANINE   Business, hah! That's what you call it?

JEAN-PIERRE   I never kiss anyone like this.

He kisses her.

JEAN-PIERRE   (*cont'd*) Or hold anyone like this. Or want to make love to anyone . . . like this . . .

She starts to melt.

JANINE   Let's go to Palm Beach tomorrow and stay in a suite at the Bel-Aire and dance on the rooftop terrace.

JEAN-PIERRE   I have a charter tomorrow.

JANINE   Oh, yes, Mrs. Steel Heiress of Palm Beach. Put her off for a day.

JEAN-PIERRE   Janine—

JANINE   Mrs. Steel Heiress, the governor's little wife, and me, we all have to take our turn, don't we?

JEAN-PIERRE   Don't you understand?

JANINE   Understand what?

Jean-Pierre starts to undress her.

JEAN-PIERRE   About us . . . about us . . . us . . . us. . . .

She succumbs to him.

51   EXT: CACA, PIRATE CAY—NIGHT
Arno and Coquina are loading their stolen salvage equipment onto the boat. Arno gets under way.

COQUINA   And they are dead—everyone?

ARNO   (*nodding*) And no one knows where the boat is, except me. Give me a hand. . . .

COQUINA   You can just go down there and take what you want?

ARNO   It's salvage. The first one there strips her—why not me?

COQUINA   But stripping the dead—

ARNO   It's a target of opportunity—and the only chance I've got to beat this rap.

52   EXT: BIMINI DOCKS—NEXT DAY
Jean-Pierre gallantly leads Mrs. Steel Heiress onto his boat. She smiles at him.

ORTEGA   Jean-Pierre!

Jean-Pierre looks over at Ortega, approaching with Juanito. Ortega's left arm is in a sling. He's alive.

JEAN-PIERRE (*to the lady*) Excuse me, *chérie.*

Jean-Pierre goes to meet Ortega on the dock.

JEAN-PIERRE (*cont'd*) I see you got fixed up fast.

Ortega brushes it off.

ORTEGA Got a job for you.

JEAN-PIERRE Sorry, I've got this charter.

ORTEGA I'll give you a better one. Last night, someone stole some stuff from a store over on Pirate Cay. The young Driscoll girl, that Coquina, was involved. You know who she's hanging around with . . . ?

JEAN-PIERRE Yeah, Arno.

ORTEGA There's big money on his head. Nobody cuts Ortega and gets away with it.

Jean-Pierre is turning something over in his brain.

JEAN-PIERRE How big?

ORTEGA Whatever the lady pays, I double it. . . . Now get going.

Ortega smiles. Jean-Pierre nods.

53 EXT: LAGOON—DAY
The suns beats down. Arno's boat is anchored at the wreck of the Pirate of Chicago.

Aboard the Caca, *Arno has gotten into the diving suit; it is big on him. The air lines are attached to an old converter, which is on the deck of the boat. The suit is old and stiff and is difficult to maneuver in.*

Coquina is tying a rope around his waist that will function as his life line. Arno has fitted the sledge hammer and the crowbar into the waist rope. A life-preserver ring floats on a line alongside the boat.

ANOTHER ANGLE

as Coquina helps him attach and close the hard hat, which has the air lines fitted into it.

ANGLE FROM WATER

as Arno slides over the side of the boat and lowers himself into the water.

On board, Coquina has started the converter and is playing out the rope line attached to Arno.

54 EXT: UNDERWATER—CONTINUOUS
Arno descending the wreck.

SEVERAL DIFFERENT ANGLES

of Arno slowly descending in his diving suit, air lines traveling above him, schools of colorful fish crossing his path.

Arno is unaware that the entry points of the air hoses are beginning to come loose from the hard hat.

The air hose connection and seals dislodge, for the fittings are old and not able to withstand the water.

CLOSE-UP THROUGH WINDOW OF HARD HAT

shows us that Arno is beginning to experience difficulty in getting air; water is seeping in.

MEDIUM SHOT

He is trying to reach up and adjust the air hoses, but the arms of the diving suit are restrictive.

55 EXT: BOAT—CONTINUOUS
Coquina looks down in the water. She can't see anything except rippling reflections of the sun.

56 EXT: UNDERWATER—CONTINUOUS

ANOTHER CLOSE-UP

shows us Arno having real difficulty now in being able to breathe. The air is bubbling out of the air line and into the water before it enters the helmet.

ANOTHER ANGLE

shows Arno fighting desperately now to get out of the suit and hard hat, which have become a lethal coffin.

57 EXT: BOAT—CONTINUOUS
Coquina, knowing that Arno is in trouble, pulls on the life line, trying to keep the failing generator going with one hand and pull up the rope with the other.

58 EXT: UNDERWATER—CONTINUOUS

Arno is in a desperate struggle to get out of the suit. He succeeds in freeing himself from the rope around his waist, the sledge hammer and crowbar being lost in the process.

Now he squirms and struggles and tears at the suit to get free of it. He succeeds in jettisoning his lead shoes.

CUT TO:

59 EXT: BOAT—CONTINUOUS

Coquina is pulling on the rope with both hands, but it suddenly gives as Arno releases it below, and when the unattached rope surfaces, she realizes the desperateness of Arno's situation. She flips off her shoes, sheds her dress, and dives in.

60 EXT: UNDERWATER—CONTINUOUS

Coquina plunges toward Arno.

ANOTHER ANGLE

as Coquina reaches Arno. She opens the snap locks that hold the diving suit and, as the suit opens, she flips open the clasps that hold the hard hat and pushes it off.

CLOSE SHOT

as the hard hat falls away; Coquina helps Arno free himself from the suit. Arno's eyes reflect his panic.

LONGER SHOT

as Coquina, holding Arno's hand, helps pull him toward the surface.

CUT TO:

61 EXT: SURFACE—CONTINUOUS
First Coquina comes up, then Arno. Arno is gasping, choking, not able to get his breath. Coquina pushes the life-preserver ring to him.

ANOTHER ANGLE

as Coquina reaches the boat; Arno is holding on to the life preserver. Another few seconds below water would have been the end of him. Finally his gasps straighten out into breaths and slowly he comes back together.

CLOSE-UP—ARNO

Nose bloody, face angry.

ARNO They'll be searching soon—and the hell of it is I can't get in and I can't get away. The birds are getting more off her than I am.

Angry, he picks up the generator and throws it over the side.

ANOTHER ANGLE

as Coquina comes to Arno with a wet towel and tenderly wipes blood from his nose. Arno slumps into the chair behind the wheel.

He reaches into his pocket and pulls out his father's watch, full of water, ruined.

ARNO *(cont'd)* Dammit!

62 EXT: WATERS NEAR THE WRECK SITE—LATE AFTER-NOON

Jean-Pierre's boat appears. He is reading the chart and exploring the lagoons. Janine is unhappy, tired, parched.

JANINE   Give up, Jean-Pierre. There's three hundred islands.

JEAN-PIERRE   Then we'll do three hundred.

JANINE   What are you really up to?

JEAN-PIERRE   Get me something to drink.

JANINE   Get it yourself.

63   EXT: ON BOARD CACA—LATE AFTERNOON
Coquina is pouring rum into a glass for Arno, who sits with his back against the steering box, in his swim trunks, his father's watch still in his hand.

Arno takes a long drink of the rum, feels its restorative effect, looks at her.

ARNO   My father came to America, worked hard, saved his money, put me through college. Like everyone, he invested everything in stocks; then, when things crashed, lost all he had. He couldn't take it. He hanged himself in the basement of the house he no longer owned. After the grave-side service ended, I went straight to the airport, took the first plane going anywhere, wound up here. Only thing I brought with me: his watch. I drove an ambulance in the war and saved lives every day, but I couldn't save my own family. That's why I'm here. I didn't want anything to do with a world that could do that to a man.

COQUINA   Then why are you doing this?

ARNO   Well, maybe I've overcome everything except tempta-
tion.

ANOTHER ANGLE

*as Arno gets up, goes to his engine, begins to detach a metal
handle.*

ARNO   (*cont'd*) You can hook a marlin or hook a few diamonds and emeralds. It's all fair game.

*He has taken off the handle, which he weighs up and down for
heft.*

COQUINA   Let's go, Arno. Let's just report it and leave it alone.
It's not yours.

ARNO   I had nothing to do with the death of these people. Now
someone will strip what's on her, and that someone is going
to be me—us.

COQUINA   Us?

ARNO   (*smiling at her*) Us. Money will help us to get where
we're going.

64   EXT: JEAN-PIERRE'S BOAT—CONTINUOUS
Jean-Pierre is at the top controls using his binoculars.

JEAN-PIERRE   Janine, get up here. Take a look. Hurry!

She's sullen. He hands her the binoculars.

JEAN-PIERRE   (*cont'd*) That his boat? The *Caca*?

JANINE   Looks like it. So what?

JEAN-PIERRE   So we pay him a visit.

JANINE   For the reward money. . . .

JEAN-PIERRE   No, my sweet. Something better.

Janine now understands Jean-Pierre's motive.

JANINE   Even if he's found it, you think Arno's going to let you in on it?

JEAN-PIERRE   Why not? You know me, Janine.

JANINE   Yes. And I know Arno.

JEAN-PIERRE   So?

JANINE   So.

65   EXT: *CACA*—LATE AFTERNOON—CONTINUOUS

COQUINA   You shouldn't go down again.

ARNO   One last try. If I don't bust the glass, we clear out of here.

ANOTHER ANGLE FROM THE WATER—CONTINUOUS

as Arno dives, the camera moves up and holds on Coquina's anxious face.

CUT TO:

66   EXT: UNDERWATER—CONTINUOUS
Arno plummeting toward wreckage.

ANOTHER ANGLE

as Arno approaches porthole.

TIGHT SHOT ON PORTHOLE

as Arno, holding on, his face grimly determined, pounds on the glass with the handle. But the bigger the effort, the more resistance he gets from the water. Now, out of breath, frustrated, angry, his nose bleeding profusely, he kicks off the hull toward the surface.

CUT TO:

67 EXT: SURFACE—CONTINUOUS
Arno surfaces at the boat. Coquina reaches over the side and holds him as he tries to restore his breathing. Blood pours from his nose. He is completely beat.

CLOSE-UP—ARNO

Nose bloody, face angry.

Sudden sound of a high-powered boat engine entering the cove. Arno raises his head.

68 EXT: SURFACE—ARNO'S POV
The tricolore is flapping in the stern of Jean-Pierre's boat.

69 EXT: CACA—CONTINUOUS
TWO SHOT—ARNO AND COQUINA

Arno shakes his head, Coquina nods in understanding.

ANOTHER ANGLE

as Arno tosses the bloody towel under the chair.

Jean-Pierre pulls alongside, cuts engine.

ANOTHER ANGLE

emphasizing Janine giving Coquina the once-over. Jean-Pierre holds on to Arno's boat, keeping them fast.

JEAN-PIERRE I'm glad to find you.

ARNO Yeah? Looking for the reward?

JEAN-PIERRE Reward?

ARNO You kill a guy and run, there's a reward.

JEAN-PIERRE Oh, yeah. But I don't come for that reward. There's a bigger prize. I think maybe you have found something—have you?

ARNO Like what?

Arno turns his head, tries to wipe away the blood that continues to ooze from his nose without Jean-Pierre seeing it.

JEAN-PIERRE That which makes your nose bleed.

ARNO This? I got smacked by the butt of my rod.

ANOTHER ANGLE

as Jean-Pierre comes onto Arno's boat.

JEAN-PIERRE   Wherever it is, Arno, you can't do it alone.

ARNO   Do what alone? The sun's got you, J.-P.

JEAN-PIERRE   Don't be greedy. From what the radio says, we can both have plenty.

ARNO   Whatever you're talking about, you can have it all. Now, shove off. Coquina and I came here to be alone.

Janine makes eye contact with Coquina.

JEAN-PIERRE   Let me explain why you need me for a partner. Number one, there is a big search on—boats, planes—you have very little time. Number two, they're looking for you, so you can't show your face. They buried Ortega today. Big funeral.

Janine glances at Jean-Pierre.

JEAN-PIERRE   (*cont'd*) Number three, you need equipment to go down and get what's there. I got everything you need. So that's the deal—you tell me where, I show you how, we split fifty-fifty.

Arno is silent.

JEAN-PIERRE   (*cont'd*) Another thing. Deal or no deal, wherever your boat goes, mine goes.

Arno hesitates as he weighs all this.

JEAN-PIERRE   (*cont'd*) Oh, come on, Arno. So there'll be two rich men instead of one.

Arno (Benjamin Bratt) lives alone with his parrot, Dorothy, and scavenges the beaches for a living.

Not only does Arno have to deal with those who are searching for him, but also with the intrigue that exists between him, Jean-Pierre's wife, Janine (Simone-Élise Girard), and Coquina (Mili Avital)

Arno, his nose bloodied from deep-diving to the wreck, is still intent on reaching its treasures.

Arno can reach the wreck but not the treasure.

Arno's nemesis, Jean-Pierre (Armand Assante), has succeeded in infiltrating Arno's secret.

Coquina, who has come back into Arno's life, is the only one he can trust—or can he?

He puts out his hand to shake. Arno looks at him, looks at his hand.

ARNO   You got a diving suit?

JEAN-PIERRE   In the forward hold. Janine . . .

She opens the hold, takes out a diving suit. Holds it up.

ARNO   How about a generator? Mine kicked the bucket.

Jean-Pierre points to an auxiliary mobile generator.

JEAN-PIERRE   You forget I hire for salvage.

ARNO   (*introducing them*) You remember Coquina—

JEAN-PIERRE   Of course, but she was not so grown-up.

JANINE   (*with a little bite*) Or so beautiful.

JEAN-PIERRE   So, come clean, Arno. Where is it?

ARNO   (*pointing*) Dead center. Must have got caught in t
he eye of the storm and tore itself open on those rocks at the
    lagoon entrance.

JEAN-PIERRE   And it's still there?

ARNO   All of it—bloody all of it—and we gotta get there be-
    fore anyone else.

70 EXT: WRECK SITE—THE NEXT MORNING
Jean-Pierre's boat and Arno's boat are rafted together, anchored

above the wreck. Aboard Jean-Pierre's boat, Arno is getting ready to go down. He wears the new diving suit.

Janine and Coquina help fit the hard hat over Arno's head and fasten it to the body of the suit.

JEAN-PIERRE   I've got a perforated eardrum. Never learned how to swim, or I'd be down there with you.

ARNO   Sure you would.

ANGLE FROM WATER

as they help Arno ease over the side of the boat and enter the water. He has a small sledge hammer and a crowbar stuck inside the rope at his waist.

Jean-Pierre starts up the generator. Coquina and Janine begin to play out the air hose.

Arno disappears from the surface.

71   EXT: UNDERWATER—MOMENTS LATER
Arno descends toward a porthole.

In the salon window, a woman's face is visible through the glass. Arno takes the sledge hammer, raps it against the glass. Cracks but doesn't break. Tries several times.

Arno turns the sledge hammer around (this is a small hammer with a short handle) and thrusts the end of the handle against the glass. It shatters. Arno pokes away all the glass, now has access to the people he can reach inside. He returns the sledge hammer to his waist rope and reaches in.

ANOTHER ANGLE

as Arno begins to strip the jewelry from the fat woman at the porthole. The diving suit has sleeves that fit to his wrists with elastic, leaving his hands free. He removes earrings, necklace, clusters of bracelets on each of the woman's wrists, emerald brooches from her dress.

Another angle as Arno tackles the rings on the woman's hands. He has great difficulty getting them off her fat, swollen fingers, especially one ring, shown in close-up, which features an enormous diamond.

Arno puts the jewelry into a small pouch that is built into the front of his diving suit.

72 EXT: UNDERWATER—ANOTHER ANGLE FROM OUT-SIDE BOAT—CONTINUOUS

Arno goes to another porthole and breaks it open. The body nearest him is obviously that of a waiter. Arno pushes him away to get at a woman he can barely reach. After several tries, he finally gets his fingers on her dress and pulls her over to him. She is laden with jewels, and Arno methodically strips her.

Only now, instead of putting the loot in the small pouch, Arno slips the jewels in the sleeve of the diving suit, hiding them.

Arno pushes his arm through the porthole as far as it will go.

Inside the boat, his arm waves around, fishing for jeweled bodies. Inches from his arm, a LARGE SHARK hovers, watching.

Arno pulls his arm from the porthole, unaware of the shark, unable to reach any bodies.

Arno looks through the porthole one last time, when suddenly the shark pushes its head through the porthole. Arno screams and quickly backs away.

The shark can't fit through the porthole and disappears inside the boat.

Arno quickly tugs his life line and is pulled to the surface.

73 EXT: JEAN-PIERRE'S BOAT—LATER
Arno empties the contents of his pouch. His helmet is off, and Jean-Pierre, Janine, and Coquina are clustered around the chart table on which the valuables are being placed.

Each person, in turn, as a piece of jewelry is passed, looks in wonderment at the treasure, almost reverentially.

Coquina picks up an ornate necklace of diamonds, emeralds, and rubies, the jewels sparkling in the sun.

COQUINA   I have never seen diamonds like this before.

JANINE   And now that you have seen them?

COQUINA   They have a certain beauty.

Arno reaches over, takes the necklace from her, holds it against her.

ARNO   (*admiringly*) The queen!

In the distance is the sound of airplanes. All of them look up toward the sun.

CUT TO:

74 EXT: SKY—CONTINUOUS
Two low-flying planes are in the distance.

75 EXT: JEAN-PIERRE'S BOAT—CONTINUOUS
Jean-Pierre has binoculars trained on the airplanes.

JEAN-PIERRE Search planes.

He puts down the binoculars, reaches over, takes the necklace from around Coquina's neck, and returns it to the table.

JEAN-PIERRE *(cont'd)* They may be looking for you. Everybody know your boat.

76 EXT: A BEACH NEAR A LAGOON—SUNSET
The planes are nowhere to be seen or heard.

Jean-Pierre takes his boat to one side of the beach, where there is considerable vegetation.

Arno takes his boat to the opposite side of the beach and maneuvers it right in among some mangroves.

Jean-Pierre and Janine cut branches and foliage, which they lay across their boat for camouflage from the air search.

Arno, helped by Coquina, is also camouflaging his boat by using beach vegetation.

77 EXT: JEAN-PIERRE'S BOAT—NIGHT
Thoroughly camouflaged.

78 INT: JEAN-PIERRE'S BOAT
Jean-Pierre, Arno, Coquina, and Janine sit around the cabin

table, on which is heaped the booty taken from the wreck. Bottle of rum and glasses on the table. Jean-Pierre has a magnifying glass, through which he's looking at a bracelet.

Jean-Pierre puts down the magnifying glass, shoves two bracelets and two rings toward Arno, and pulls the ornate necklace toward himself.

JEAN-PIERRE   Okay, the necklace for two bracelets and these two rings.

ARNO   How about the other way around? Will you take what you give?

JEAN-PIERRE   It's just . . . I have a use for the necklace.

ARNO   What, to wear with your evening gowns?

Jean-Pierre picks two rings from the center pile and puts them in front of Arno.

JEAN-PIERRE   All right, Arno, I'll throw in two more rings.

ARNO   I've been counting. There are more diamonds in one strand of the necklace than in all the other stuff combined.

JEAN-PIERRE   But the diamonds of the rings are of much higher quality—and more carats.

ARNO   Then you take them.

JEAN-PIERRE   That's not the idea. . . . Listen, I deserve the choice since I've got to run the risk of fencing them. You can't be seen because you're wanted for murder.

Janine looks at Jean-Pierre, realizing he's lying about Ortega.

ARNO I found the wreck.

ANOTHER ANGLE

as Arno picks up the necklace and holds it at Coquina's throat.

CLOSE-UP

of Arno as he looks at the beauty of the necklace against Coquina's throat, then raises his eyes to the beauty of her face.

ARNO *(cont'd)* I definitely want the necklace.

Arno turns his eyes from Coquina and looks at Jean-Pierre. The two men try to stare each other down.

JEAN-PIERRE So do I.

COQUINA Do you know what we do here to decide things?

She takes a nut from a bowl, cracks the shell in two, takes out the kernel, puts it under one of the shells.

COQUINA *(cont'd)* If you choose the shell with the kernel, the necklace is yours.

She shuffles the shells.

ANGLE-TIGHT SHOT

that accentuates the two men, a long beat intercut with close-ups as Jean-Pierre studies the shells. Arno watches him closely, keeping his eyes on Jean-Pierre, not looking at the shells.

Jean-Pierre starts to reach for a shell, then hesitates.

JEAN-PIERRE *(nervously)* Do it once again, Coquina.

Coquina shuffles the shells again.

Jean-Pierre finally touches one shell with his forefinger. Coquina turns it over: no kernel.

CLOSE-UP

of Jean-Pierre's dejection. Arno, smiling, picks up the necklace.

ARNO Now it's your turn.

Jean-Pierre glares at Arno and angrily plucks a bracelet from the heap.

ARNO *(cont'd)* *(to Coquina)* You choose for us.

COQUINA But, Arno . . .

ARNO Go ahead.

Janine fumes as Coquina and Jean-Pierre take turns in making selections from the heap.

Once or twice, on Jean-Pierre's turn, Janine stops him and points to another piece, and he changes his selection.

Arno sits back, watching Coquina with a look of wry amusement on his face. Coquina picks up a pair of earrings as if they might break, studying their glistening beauty.

79 INT: JEAN-PIERRE'S BOAT—LATER
Jean-Pierre makes the final pick, then sits back and studies Arno.

JEAN-PIERRE You sure that's all of it?

ARNO What do you mean by that?

JEAN-PIERRE Well, there was no one down there to watch you. . . .

ARNO Why don't you dive tomorrow?

JEAN-PIERRE If I could swim, I would.

ARNO Then you'll just have to trust me, dearie.

JEAN-PIERRE Speaking of trust, I think we should have some insurance against unexpected departure. (*holds up a small engine part*) I took this off your engine.

ARNO (*holding up a small engine part*) And I took this off yours.

Jean-Pierre steams.

80 EXT: ARNO'S BOAT—THAT NIGHT
Candles burning, the jewelry between them with a bottle of rum and glasses, Arno raises his glass to Coquina.

Coquina raises her glass in turn.

COQUINA And here's a little something to go with your drink.

She puts the nut from the shell in his mouth.

ARNO   What? You mean . . . both shells were empty?

COQUINA   A trick we learn as children.

ARNO   No wonder I love you.

He draws her to him and kisses her deeply, then slowly, sensuously, bedecks her with some of the jewelry.

The jewelry and the moment excite her. She draws him toward the mattress spread out on the deck and they lie down. Arno suddenly stops.

ARNO   (*cont'd*) You know, it occurred to me.

COQUINA   What?

ARNO   That the more I bring up, the less I'm needed.

COQUINA   What a thing to say.

ARNO   Think about it. What's to keep Jean-Pierre from taking off, radioing the Constable, or cutting off my air supply?

COQUINA   Arno!

ARNO   Well, it's true.

COQUINA   *I* need you.

ARNO   You do?

She looks into his eyes deeply.

COQUINA   Yes, I do. So you'll be safe.

They make love, their first time. It's almost a dream. The exotic surroundings at night, the lovers, their hands, their faces, the overhanging trees, the water, the moon. Arno falls into a haze of passion.

DISSOLVE TO:

81   EXT: ARNO'S BOAT—LATER THAT NIGHT
Arno and Coquina lie under the stars in their mosquito-net cocoon. Coquina snuggles in his arms. He takes his father's broken watch and drapes it around her neck.

COQUINA   This is all so fast, Arno.

ARNO   Some things are meant to be.

Coquina holds the watch, now around her neck, in her hand.

COQUINA   And we're meant to be?

ARNO   Oh, yes.

She kisses him deeply.

82   EXT: JEAN-PIERRE'S BOAT—THE NEXT DAY
Arno picks up the hard hat.

ARNO   I'm going to try to get into the boat, if the resident shark'll let me.

COQUINA   We have enough, Arno.

Arno holds up his dagger.

ARNO I'll be okay.

JEAN-PIERRE We want all the jewelry, don't we?

ANGLE

as Arno fits the hard hat on his head and Jean-Pierre fastens it to the body of the suit.

JEAN-PIERRE (*cont'd*) Pay attention to the air lines and rope—
we've got to be able to pull you free.

ANOTHER ANGLE

Arno and Coquina as Arno prepares to go over the side.

COQUINA Be careful.

Arno smiles at her, nods. He makes sure the dagger is at his side.

83 EXT: UNDERWATER—MOMENTS LATER
Long shot of Arno as, holding on to his waist rope, he starts to descend along the hull of the wreck.

CLOSER SHOT

of Arno descending. During all these underwater sequences, there are schools of spectacular fish, some of indescribable brilliance, some of awesome proportions like the jewfish.

In this descent, Arno meets a constant stream of these fish, but suddenly, as he floats upward, he is jerked to one side.

CUT TO:

84   EXT: JEAN-PIERRE'S BOAT—CONTINUOUS
There is the sound of distant planes as the others look toward the sky.

JEAN-PIERRE   They're headed this way. Let's pull him up.

Jean-Pierre and Janine start to pull up on the rope line. Coquina is monitoring the generator.

85   EXT: UNDERWATER—MOMENTS LATER
SERIES OF ANGLES

as Arno moves along the hull of the ship to its underside where the deck is located.

Arno works his way across the deck to the ship's doors. He tries unsuccessfully to open them, the impact of the crash having jammed them.

ANOTHER ANGLE

shows us that his air lines have become tangled on the wreck, stopping his descent. He jerks on the line twice.

86   EXT: JEAN-PIERRE'S BOAT—CONTINUOUS

COQUINA   Stop! Stop! Look at the lines.

Jean-Pierre eases the lines out.

JEAN-PIERRE   The planes are getting closer!

87   EXT: UNDERWATER—CONTINUOUS

Arno's struggles back to the wreck and slowly unwraps the lines from their tangle.

He has to go very slowly, because the lines are wrapped around a sharp piece of metal. A rip or puncture is all too easy to make.

88 EXT: JEAN-PIERRE'S BOAT—MOMENTS LATER
The planes drone closer, flying low.

JEAN-PIERRE All right, let's all go below.

Coquina hesitates.

JEAN-PIERRE *(cont'd)* Now! He'll be all right.

Jean-Pierre and Janine pull Coquina down into the cabin.

89 INT: JEAN-PIERRE'S BOAT—CONTINUOUS
Jean-Pierre holds Coquina tight, despite her protests. She doesn't want to leave Arno alone.

90 EXT: UNDERWATER—CONTINUOUS
Arno can't untangle the lines and is getting no help from above. He's not getting enough air. Arno pulls on his life line. He wants up.

91 INT: JEAN-PIERRE'S BOAT—HOLD
From inside the boat, Coquina can see the life line being tugged by Arno from below.

COQUINA There's something wrong.

But there is still the sound of the plane droning above. Jean-Pierre holds her back.

JEAN-PIERRE Not yet!

92 EXT: UNDERWATER—CONTINUOUS
Arno is definitely losing air and is in danger of suffocating. He is getting weak. He tugs furiously on the life line.

93 INT: JEAN-PIERRE'S BOAT—HOLD
Coquina can hear the plane flying away, and she breaks free of Jean-Pierre, rushing to Arno's life line. Jean-Pierre gives Janine a smile, and she meets his gaze coldly.

JEAN-PIERRE *(to Janine)* What?

94 EXT: JEAN-PIERRE'S BOAT—CONTINUOUS
Coquina begins to help play the lines, saving Arno once again.

95 EXT: UNDERWATER—CONTINUOUS
Arno takes deep breaths of the air as it hisses into his helmet. He's safe.

96 EXT: BEACH—CACA—NIGHT
Bright moon. The Caca is at its mooring on its side of the beach.

97 INT: ABOARD CACA—NIGHT
Coquina and Arno, alone.

ARNO You saved my life again, Pirate Princess.

They kiss.

ARNO *(cont'd)* You're making me break my rule.

COQUINA What rule?

ARNO   Not to want anything.

He holds a diamond ring to her finger.

COQUINA   What do you want?

ARNO   To leave here—with you.

He slips the ring on her finger.

COQUINA   Then let's do it.

ARNO   Now?

COQUINA   How much do we need?

Arno looks at her.

COQUINA   (*cont'd*) We could quit now with what we've got, couldn't we? We've more than enough. It's getting dangerous.

ARNO   What do you mean?

COQUINA   You should have seen how Jean-Pierre was looking at you today. He might turn you in for the price on your head.

Arno thinks this over carefully.

COQUINA   (*cont'd*) I'm scared to fall in love with you. I don't know who you are, Arno. You say you don't care about worldly things, but you're risking your life for jewels.

ARNO With all this, we can live well. Things'll be simple. You won't be scared anymore.

COQUINA Let's leave now, while we can. Before there is more trouble. Please?

Arno smiles.

He scoops up the jewelry into a bag.

COQUINA *(cont'd)* Where are we going?

ARNO To take care of a murder rap.

98 EXT: WATER—MOMENTS LATER
Arno helps Coquina into the Caca's skiff. Arno takes a paddle from the bottom of the skiff, starts silently to scull them away from the beach.

CUT TO:

99 EXT: OPEN SEA—SKIFF—NIGHT
Outboard operating now, going full tilt.

CUT TO:

100 EXT: BIMINI STREET—NIGHT
Arno and Coquina go down Bimini Street, sticking to the shadows, trying not to be seen.

101 INT: SILVER SLIPPER BAR—THAT NIGHT
Willie the piano player is in the middle of a number when Coquina enters the bar.

Mama Nima notices Coquina at the door. From the rear, the Constable also sees Coquina. He finishes his drink and approaches her.

CONSTABLE   Ah, Coquina . . . sit down. We must talk—

COQUINA   Arno wants to see you.

CONSTABLE   Where is he?

COQUINA   In your office.

102   INT: CONSTABLE'S OFFICE—MOMENTS LATER
Arno is in the office as the Constable enters.

ARNO   I want to make bail.

CONSTABLE   You? You have any idea how much the bail
would be?

ARNO   Well, I know killing is a capital offense . . .

CONSTABLE   . . . way beyond you.

ANOTHER ANGLE

*as Arno puts his hand in his pocket and draws out the bracelet
he had hidden in the sleeve of his diving suit. He tosses it on
the desk in front of the Constable. The Constable looks at the
bracelet, looks at Arno, picks up the bracelet, inspects it closely.*

CONSTABLE   (*cont'd*) Well, now, that ought to do it . . .

Stands up.

CONSTABLE   (*cont'd*) . . . but we'll have to reduce the offense.

ANOTHER ANGLE

as the Constable goes to the door of his office, which opens into the Silver Slipper, from the Constable's POV. The Constable can see the bar with several men standing at it.

CONSTABLE *(cont'd)* Hey, Chino, Merimac, come here!

ANGLE FROM INSIDE OFFICE

as the Constable returns to his desk and the two deputies, half tanked, come into the room.

CONSTABLE *(cont'd)* Close the door.

Merimac closes the door. He recognizes Arno and reacts.

CONSTABLE *(cont'd)* Raise your right hands.

Merimac and Chino stand in front of the Constable's desk with their right hands raised.

CONSTABLE *(cont'd)* You both saw the fight between Ortega and Arno and you do solemnly swear that Ortega came at Arno with an ax and Arno wounded him in self-defense.

MERIMAC Yep.

Chino nods.

CONSTABLE *(giving them each a dollar)* Here you are.

They take their dollars, leave.

As the Constable signs a piece of paper which he hands to Arno.

CONSTABLE *(cont'd)* You're all set.

Arno takes the paper, starts to leave, does a double take.

ARNO Wait a minute. You said "wounded"?

CONSTABLE It was only a flesh wound. . . . You didn't know? I thought Jean-Pierre—

Arno gives Coquina a sharp look that doesn't escape the Constable, then takes a pair of diamond earrings from his pocket and puts them on the desk.

ARNO Future bail. See you.

Arno takes Coquina's arm and leads her quickly through the door.

The Constable picks up the earrings, looks at them. Picks up the telephone.

CONSTABLE Ortega? A little bee just flew in here. It's time to go looking for the hive; and I bet you'll find Jean-Pierre in the honey.

103 EXT: BIMINI STREETS—LATER

ARNO That frog bastard Jean-Pierre. He knew about Ortega!

COQUINA Those jewels you gave the Constable—they weren't part of the split with Jean-Pierre, were they?

Arno gives her a look, doesn't answer.

COQUINA (*cont'd*) I don't remember seeing them. . . .

ARNO They were part of the split while I was under water.

COQUINA But that's dishonest.

ARNO Not telling me about Ortega—that's honest? He wanted me to risk my life; then he'd steal the loot, go back to Bimini, because as long as I thought I was a wanted man I'd stay away.

COQUINA What are you going to do?

ARNO Are you with me?

COQUINA How can I trust you? You don't trust anyone.

ARNO You know my motto? Keep your hands in your pockets, your flanks covered, and never sleep in strange beds.

Coquina doesn't know how to feel.

ARNO (*cont'd*) Let's get going.

104 EXT: JEAN-PIERRE'S BOAT—NEXT DAY
Low-flying planes are heard in the distance. The women are below. Arno and Jean-Pierre grab fishing poles and pretend to fish at the sound of a plane overhead.

JEAN-PIERRE It's about time we close down.

ARNO Then I can pack up and escape the murder rap.

JEAN-PIERRE Absolutely. Take your share and run.

ARNO Why would I do that, J.P.?

JEAN-PIERRE What do you mean?

ARNO Ortega's a *walking* corpse, isn't he?

Music is heard from belowdecks.

JEAN-PIERRE What do you talk about?

ARNO You and your dirty friends.

Jean-Pierre looks at him.

ARNO (*cont'd*) He's alive. And you knew.

JEAN-PIERRE Where did you hear this?

ARNO Right from Constable Jim's mouth.

JEAN-PIERRE You went to the Constable? When? How?

ARNO You thought I'd never find out, didn't you?

Jean-Pierre leaps up.

JEAN-PIERRE You're crazy! They probably followed you! They know where we are!

Arno leaps up.

ARNO You let me think I was a murderer!

JEAN-PIERRE Ortega! Everyone! I'm a dead man!

ARNO   I hope so.

Jean-Pierre leaps at Arno, and Arno knocks him down.

Jean-Pierre scrambles to his feet and a fierce fight ensues, ending when Arno lands a heavy punch, catapulting Jean-Pierre overboard.

Jean-Pierre flails about in the water, gasping, thrashing about.

JEAN-PIERRE   I can't swim!

ARNO   Good time to learn.

JEAN-PIERRE   My ear! . . . Arno! Please . . . I can't . . . Save me. . . . There's gold. . . .

ARNO   What?

JEAN-PIERRE   In the safe—

Jean-Pierre goes under, fights his way up.

JEAN-PIERRE   *(cont'd)* Arno, gold!

Jean-Pierre goes under.

ARNO   Another dirty secret.

JEAN-PIERRE   *(gasping as he surfaces)* Please, Arno, we can . . . trust me!

He goes under for the third time. It looks like he's going to drown.

Arno still hesitates, then dives in.

105 EXT: JEAN-PIERRE'S BOAT—NIGHT
Jean-Pierre lights a dazzling display of flares mounted on the outriggers, which shoot a fountain of sparks over the water.

106 EXT: UNDERWATER—CONTINUOUS
Arno descends in the shimmering light provided by the fountain of sparks above the water.

107 INT: UNDERWATER—SUNKEN YACHT
The fountain of sparks above the water surface provides shimmering light to the dark water.

Arno is moving inside the sunken yacht, holding an underwater lantern, which illuminates very little. He reaches the open door to the Purser's office.

REVERSE ANGLE

as Arno enters the office. Some office furniture and supplies are floating around, but the desk and chairs are in place, since they were fastened to the floor.

ANOTHER ANGLE

as he moves through the room to the rear wall where there is a large safe set in the wall. The bodies of the Purser and a Deck Officer are floating around.

Tight shot of Arno at the safe. He tries the handle but it is securely locked. He takes his jimmy bar from his waist rope and tries to get a hold with it, but cannot.

Arno suddenly freezes. He aims his light beam on the door.

108 INT: UNDERWATER—SUNKEN YACHT—CONTINUOUS
ANOTHER ANGLE

The huge SHARK, *swimming by in the corridor, is seen through the glass panels on the other side of the door.*

Tight shot of Arno not moving, hoping the shark will not notice him and swim on.

ANOTHER ANGLE

Arno motionless as the shark swims ominously outside the door.

CUT TO:

109 INT: JEAN-PIERRE'S BOAT—CABIN—CONTINUOUS
Janine is topside, on the lookout for any approaching vessels.

On deck, Jean-Pierre tends the generator. Coquina has her hands on the rope coil, feeding it to keep it from fouling.

JEAN-PIERRE (*low voice*) How much is Arno giving you?

COQUINA Giving me?

JEAN-PIERRE What share of the split?

COQUINA I don't know, we're together.

Another angle as he studies her for a beat.

JEAN-PIERRE You could wind up with nothing.

Coquina is suspicious of him.

JEAN-PIERRE   (*cont'd*) I will propose something—where does he hide his stuff, do you know?

COQUINA   No.

JEAN-PIERRE   Find out and I split it with you, half and half. That way you know what you get. Find out.

COQUINA   I trust Arno.

JEAN-PIERRE   There may be complications for you about Arno.

COQUINA   Like what?

JEAN-PIERRE   Like maybe he takes up again with my wife and you get nothing.

Close-up of Coquina's reaction. Does he really have something going, or is it Jean-Pierre's ploy?

CUT TO:

110   INT: UNDERWATER—WRECK—PURSER'S OFFICE
The SHARK is gone. Arno goes cautiously to the door, inspects the area.

Arno is about to leave the office when the shark appears from out of nowhere and slams into him, knocking him down, and knifes into the room.

Arno struggles back to his feet. He pulls out his dagger.

The line tightens and Arno starts to move as the shark turns to attack. Arno has the dagger ready in hand. The shark attacks.

ANOTHER ANGLE

as Arno jabs the dagger into the shark's nose, causing it to veer away, but it turns with great speed and attacks again. Arno again jabs at the nose of the shark but its swinging body slams against him, ripping off his waist rope.

The dagger swirls away. Arno, desperate now, dives for the door as the shark turns for another run at him.

ANGLE FROM DOOR

as the shark attacks. Arno has reached the door, gets through it, shuts it as the shark comes slamming into it. The impact batters Arno, but he recovers and closes the door, imprisoning the shark in the purser's office.

There is a huge tear in his suit, which fills with water.

111 EXT: ON DECK—CONTINUOUS

JEAN-PIERRE   (*to Coquina*) How about Arno doesn't come up. The generator conks out. And his share is all ours.

The generator suddenly stops.

Coquina tries to get to the switch.

COQUINA   No! No! You can't do that!

He stops her as Janine comes down from topside.

JANINE   What's going on?

COQUINA   He did something!

JEAN-PIERRE   I did nothing.

She's frantic. He's restraining her from getting to the generator.

JEAN-PIERRE   (*cont'd*) It's an old generator! You'll break it.

Coquina grabs at the switch. Jean-Pierre pushes her away and kneels down by the generator, looking carefully for what's wrong.

JANINE   (*to Jean-Pierre*) Get it started. None of your dirty tricks.

COQUINA   (*to Janine*) He did something.

JEAN-PIERRE   Nonsense, look for yourself.

COQUINA   Arno will die.

Janine is panicking.

JANINE   What the hell did you do?

JEAN-PIERRE   Nothing, I tell—

JANINE   The devil you didn't.

She pushes by Jean-Pierre and turns a switch on the generator. The generator sputters to life.

112 EXT: WRECK—CONTINUOUS
Arno is semiconscious, the shark battering the door. He works

himself out of his suit and helmet and swims desperately. The waist line is ascending as Arno swims up to it, grabs hold.

CUT TO:

113   EXT: ON DECK—CONTINUOUS

COQUINA   *(as she winds the winch)* He's on the line again!

Arno surfaces. Jean-Pierre and Janine pull him into the boat. He is spent.

JEAN-PIERRE   The suit . . . your helmet . . . what happened?

ARNO   We've got to blow the safe! You got anything?

JEAN-PIERRE   Nothing.

114   EXT: ABOARD JEAN-PIERRE'S BOAT—MOMENTS LATER
Coquina is coiling the air lines. In the background, Jean-Pierre is removing the camouflage from Arno's boat.

115   EXT: BEACH—CONTINUOUS
Janine catches up to Arno as he crosses the beach to his boat.

JANINE   Be careful! He's out of control. I'm afraid.

ARNO   Don't worry, I'm a step ahead of him.

JANINE   Don't be so sure.

ARNO   I'm sure.

116 EXT: ABOARD CACA—NIGHT
The Caca is under way, going full tilt.

Cut to Arno at the wheel. Jean-Pierre stands beside him, smoking, looking forward. The radio is playing a Bahamian song, "Big Man in the Harbor."

JEAN-PIERRE What's his name?

ARNO Orthwell.

JEAN-PIERRE We can trust him?

ARNO A helluva lot more than I trust you.

CUT TO:

117 EXT: JEAN-PIERRE'S BOAT—NIGHT
In its camouflaged position in the cove.

118 INT: JEAN-PIERRE'S BOAT—CABIN—NIGHT
Janine is in the process of modeling her clothes for Coquina. She has on a slinky, severely cut, clinging dress (highest style of the mid-thirties).

JANINE You like? I was going to wear this in Palm Beach. We were going on holiday.

COQUINA It's beautiful.

ANOTHER ANGLE

as Janine slinks over to her closet, takes out a lush fur wrap, slings it around her, and struts in it for Coquina.

JANINE   You never see something like this, eh?

COQUINA   Only in the movies.

Janine wraps it around Coquina's shoulders.

JANINE   *Voilà!* The ladies who come here never look like this. They only dress this way in civilized places—Paris, New York, London. . . .

COQUINA   Palm Beach?

JANINE   Oh, yes, Palm Beach!

Janine takes a long white silk dress out of her closet and hands it to Coquina.

JANINE   (*cont'd*) Try this one on.

Coquina takes it, holds it in front of her.

119   EXT: OMINOUS AREA—ALICE TOWN—NIGHT
Arno and Jean-Pierre approach Papa Ray's. They enter.

120   INT: PAPA RAY'S—CONTINUOUS
Papa Ray's is a dark native bar in the back streets of Alice Town. Orthwell sits at a table. Arno goes to him.

ORTHWELL   Hello, Arno.

They shake hands. Arno hands Orthwell a box.

ARNO   I brought you some of your favorite Baby Coronas— one missing.

He indicates the one he's got in his pocket. Orthwell takes them.

ORTHWELL   Thanks. My tobacco supply ain't what it used to be.

ARNO   This is Jean-Pierre—Orthwell.

Jean-Pierre and Orthwell shake hands.

121   INT: JEAN-PIERRE'S BOAT—CABIN
Janine sits in a chair.

Standing before her is Coquina, beautifully dressed in the white silk gown. Coquina is self-conscious but at the same time rather overwhelmed with the feel of the silk and the elegance of the gown.

122   INT: PAPA RAY'S—LATER
Arno, Jean-Pierre, and Orthwell with drinks. They smoke: Arno the little cigar, Jean-Pierre a pipe.

ARNO   We need some underwater bang, heavy enough to blow steel.

ORTHWELL   You remember how to use this stuff?

ARNO   It's the same?

ORTHWELL   Yes. I've got—but it costs.

ARNO   That's okay. J.-P. here is loaded.

Jean-Pierre gives him a withering look.

ARNO (cont'd) Get it out, J.-P.

Reluctantly, Jean-Pierre thrusts his hand in his pocket, brings out his wallet.

ARNO (cont'd) Start counting.

ORTHWELL It's not for me, y'understand. It's for the organization.

                                                    CUT TO:

123 INT: JEAN-PIERRE'S BOAT—CABIN
Janine and Coquina.

Coquina is wearing an entirely different outfit from Janine's wardrobe. Janine looks at her approvingly.

COQUINA Is this silk?

JANINE Isn't it divine? And would you believe it comes from worms?

COQUINA Really?

JANINE Yes, worms, from their spit or their ca-ca—I can't remember which.

Coquina looks at Janine in the mirror.

COQUINA Do you like Arno?

JANINE Of course.

COQUINA A lot?

JANINE   Of course.

Coquina turns, catches sight of herself in the full-length mirror on the back of the cabin door. She is arrested, intrigued, rather dazzled by her own looks.

CUT TO:

124   INT: PAPA RAY'S—CONTINUOUS
Arno is inspecting a large serrated shark knife, in a sheath hanging on the wall.

Orthwell is counting money that Jean-Pierre has given him.

ARNO   What about diving gear? We lost ours.

ORTHWELL   You mean hard hat and all that? Nothing. But I can show you what we used to use sponging.

He gets up, leads them out of the bar.

125   EXT: ALLEY OUTSIDE OF PAPA RAY'S—CONTINUOUS
Orthwell points to several oil drums a short distance away in the alley.

ORTHWELL   (*indicating a bolt on top of one*) Fit the air lines in here, cut the bottom out, and so long's you keep the air coming in, that'll keep the water out.

JEAN-PIERRE   A breathing station.

ORTHWELL   So to speak.

126   INT: JEAN-PIERRE'S BOAT—CABIN

Coquina is wrapped in a full-length exquisite white fur coat, looking at herself in the mirror, turning this way and that, hugging the soft fur against her face. It covers Arno's watch, which hangs around her neck.

COQUINA   I've never *been* cold.

JANINE   Oh, no! For cold a woman could wear a blanket. No, this kind of fur has nothing to do with cold.

She takes her coat from Coquina, slings it around her own shoulders, revels in its luxurious feel.

JANINE   (*cont'd*) It has to do with perfume and silk and jewels. It's what we're all about.

She puts it back on Coquina.

COQUINA   I didn't think Jean-Pierre was so generous.

JANINE   Jean-Pierre, that nickel squeezer! These are from my *first* husband. A jerk, but a spender. It's all I can do to keep Jean-Pierre's hands off what money I have. Well, I'll tell you a secret—ten minutes after we split this stuff, I split from Jean-Pierre.

ANOTHER ANGLE

as Coquina takes off the fur, starts to take off Janine's dress.

JANINE   (*cont'd*) And you go with Arno?

COQUINA   Yes.

125

JANINE I am happy for you. But get your share. Take it from me: Don't trust anything you can't put on your back—

Coquina has removed the dress. She stands there in her cotton bra and panties, looking thoughtfully at Janine. Then she looks at the beautiful silk dress.

Janine takes a necklace from her bosom, puts it on Coquina, replacing the watch.

JANINE (*cont'd*) —or around your neck. Because you will not always be so young and beautiful.

127 EXT: BEACH—DAY
Jean-Pierre is in the top of a tree on the beach where their boats are berthed. He is scanning with a pair of high-powered binoculars. Distant sound of airplanes.

ANGLE

at base of tree. Arno looking up.

ARNO How many?

JEAN-PIERRE Two working north and one over there.

ARNO Any boats?

JEAN-PIERRE (*scanning the sea*) Just one, way off to the east.

Arno climbs the tree, joins Jean-Pierre, takes his binoculars, studies the horizon.

128 EXT: ARNO'S POV—DAY
The boat is a speck on the horizon.

129 EXT: TREE OVER JEAN-PIERRE'S BOAT—CONTINUOUS

ARNO We'd better lay low today and work tonight.

JEAN-PIERRE *D'accord*—I'd say tonight's our last chance at the gold.

130 EXT: BEACH—AFTERNOON
Hot afternoon, long shot of sun beating down. As the camera moves in toward the beach, it looks like both boats are not there, so good is the camouflage. It is only when the camera gets really close in that we begin to discern a little of the boats through the cover.

131 INT: JEAN-PIERRE'S BOAT—AFTERNOON
Jean-Pierre sits at the table with his jewelry in front of him, examining and fondling it piece by piece.

Janine is sitting desultorily in a chair, watching Jean-Pierre drooling over the jewelry, disdain written all over her face.

132 INT: ARNO'S BOAT—EVENING
Arno is cooking lunch, working over the two-burner stove. The Victrola is playing. Coquina is standing next to the stove, watching Arno.

In one of the pans is fried bananas; Arno takes out a piece with his cooking fork, gives it to Coquina.

COQUINA *(tasting it)* More sugar.

Arno starts to serve the food onto two plates that are on the galley table.

COQUINA *(cont'd)* Arno?

ARNO   (*preoccupied*) Huh?

COQUINA   Are you and Janine in love?

ARNO   What?

COQUINA   Jean-Pierre said you'll run away with her.

ARNO   A man will say anything for gold—especially a Frenchman.

COQUINA   He wants me to join him and steal your stuff.

Arno lets this sink in, then smiles.

ARNO   Good idea—you do that.

COQUINA   Do what?

ARNO   Let's turn the tables: Find out where his stash is, so we can rip *him* off. You go ahead and play Jean-Pierre's game.

COQUINA   This is getting very complicated.

ARNO   The more the merrier.

Coquina just looks at Arno. This isn't the Arno she started to love.

Arno eats his food.

Coquina shakes her head but joins in the meal.

133   EXT: JEAN-PIERRE'S BOAT—NIGHT

Anchored in the middle of the cove at the wreck site, Jean-Pierre and Arno are in the process of lowering the prepared oil drum over the side and into the water. The bottom has been cut out of it, and air lines run into the top. A rope attached to the drum runs through a winch on deck.

Coquina is working the air pump.

134 EXT: BOAT—CONTINUOUS

The oil drum enters the water and disappears, rope uncoiling in back of it.

Arno, with a rope around his waist, prepares to dive off. Tied to his waist rope are two folded burlap sacks, a tin that contains the explosives, and the jimmy, tucked inside the rope. He carries in his hand one of the underwater lamps stolen from the general store and the harpoon.

He hands Janine another lantern.

ARNO   Janine comes with me.

Janine looks at Arno with surprise.

JANINE   I do what?

ARNO   If anything should happen to me . . . with the air or anything . . .

He looks at Jean-Pierre.

ARNO   (*cont'd*) . . . Janine will be there to help me and steady the drum. It's big enough for two.

Jean-Pierre thinks, seems to change his mind.

JEAN-PIERRE Good idea! Then she can make sure you don't hide any for yourself.

ARNO (*to Jean-Pierre*) And Coquina will be on board to keep an eye on you and the generator! . . . It's okay, Janine. Tie this rope around you; you can handle the detonator.

Janine looks unsure but is soothed by Arno's glance.

Arno straps the sheathed shark knife onto his thigh and dives in. Jean-Pierre lights the flares, shooting sparks over the water.

CUT TO:

135 EXT: UNDERWATER—MOMENTS LATER
Now the darkness is lit by the shimmering light.

Arno dives down to the descending oil drum and comes up inside it. As Orthwell predicted, the drum is a breathing chamber, the air pressure keeping the water out.

Janine comes up inside the drum and joins him. They are, of course, very close.

JANINE We can make a killing, you and I. I know where he's hidden his stash. Why don't we skip out tonight, just the two of us?

ARNO Where does he keep it?

JANINE I come with the stash, Arno.

Arno thinks, then decides.

ARNO   All right, let's meet at midnight, on the beach. You bring his stuff, I'll bring mine, okay?

JANINE   And we leave? Just the two of us?

ARNO   Yes.

136   EXT: JEAN-PIERRE'S BOAT—CONTINUOUS
Coquina plays out the air lines. Jean-Pierre works the air pump. Sparks fly in the night.

JEAN-PIERRE   So, Coquina, why don't we take care of "us"?

Coquina ponders, then:

COQUINA   What do you have in mind?

137   EXT: OIL DRUM—CONTINUOUS
As Arno and Janine descend along the hull of the wreck, only the upper parts of their bodies are in the drum, so that their legs extend below the drum into the water.

138   EXT: UNDERWATER—MOMENTS LATER
With the shark knife, Arno swims over to the glass and looks into the Purser's office with his lantern.

To his dismay, he sees that the large glass window is broken. The shark is free and could be anywhere.

Arno swims back to the drum.

139   INT: THE DRUM—CONTINUOUS
Arno rises, scaring Janine.

ARNO   It's not there.

JANINE   What?

ARNO   The shark. It must have escaped. Take this.

He gives her the knife, unsheathed.

Janine looks at her feet dangling below the rim of the drum in the clear water. She is getting apprehensive.

ARNO   (*cont'd*) Don't worry. It's gone. Just stay in the drum.

He opens the explosive box, takes out a hunk of explosive, and attaches a thin wire to it. He then hooks the end of the wire coil around Janine's detonator.

140   EXT: THE DRUM—CONTINUOUS
Arno swimming to the Purser's door, with a lantern.

141   INT: PURSER'S OFFICE—CONTINUOUS

REVERSE ANGLE

as Arno comes through the door with the explosive.

142   INT: DRUM—CONTINUOUS
Janine waits alone in the drum, her feet exposed. She is getting very scared.

Something is at her feet. She jumps.

143   EXT: DRUM—CONTINUOUS
Arno enters the drum.

144 INT: DRUM—CONTINUOUS
Arno comes up underwater.

ARNO   Okay.

Relieved, Janine presses the detonator.

145 INT: PURSER'S OFFICE—CONTINUOUS
As the explosive goes off, the door of the safe is blown partially open.

146 EXT: JEAN-PIERRE'S BOAT—CONTINUOUS
Coquina is going along with Jean-Pierre's game.

They see the bubbles on the water from the explosion.

JEAN-PIERRE   Aha! Bull's eye!

147 INT: DRUM—MOMENTS LATER
Arno takes deep breaths and goes to retrieve the gold. Shaking with fear, Janine whispers the Lord's Prayer in French.

She is alone.

148 INT: PURSER'S OFFICE—CONTINUOUS
Arno swims up to the safe and uses his jimmy to pry the door back, but to his dismay he finds there is an inner door that has not been affected by the explosion.

ANOTHER ANGLE

as Arno swims back to the drum.

149 INT: DRUM—CONTINUOUS

Arno takes the remaining explosives from the tin being held by Janine.

JANINE   What's wrong?

ARNO   It's not open, and this is all we've got. If this doesn't blow it . . . good-bye gold.

150   EXT: JEAN-PIERRE'S BOAT—CONTINUOUS
Suddenly Jean-Pierre stops the generator. The air flow stops.

151   INT: DRUM—CONTINUOUS
Janine, alone, notices the air flow is shut off. What is going on?

152   EXT: JEAN-PIERRE'S BOAT—CONTINUOUS
Coquina looks at Jean-Pierre and tries to stay calm.

JEAN-PIERRE   Let's leave them on the bottom. We can come back for the gold another time.

Jean-Pierre smiles. He is testing her. Coquina frees her hands to restart the generator.

COQUINA   I think we can find something more civilized.

She drops the rope she is holding, and it starts to unwind.

153   EXT: UNDERWATER—CONTINUOUS
Arno swims toward the wall safe with the explosives.

ANOTHER ANGLE

as Arno plants the explosives in the safe.

154 INT: DRUM—CONTINUOUS
Janine is getting claustrophobic, panicked, and is about to swim from the drum.

155 EXT: JEAN-PIERRE'S BOAT—CONTINUOUS
Coquina turns the generator back on.

JEAN-PIERRE Whose side are you on?

COQUINA (*trying not to be intimidated*) I haven't decided yet.

JEAN-PIERRE Let me help you make up your mind!

He kisses her. She lets him. The sparks from the flares are flying.

156 INT: DRUM—CONTINUOUS
Arno is back inside the drum, catching his breath. Janine detonates the charge.

Explosives go off at the wall safe.

157 EXT: UNDERWATER—CONTINUOUS
Arno swims to view the result.

CLOSE SHOT

of Arno at safe, which is partially blown, but he still can't get the door open. He shines his light through the partial opening and peers in.

REVERSE ANGLE

from within the safe, with light glinting off the gold bars stacked there.

158 INT: DRUM—CONTINUOUS
Arno replenishes his breath, returns to the safe.

159 INT: PURSER'S OFFICE—UNDERWATER—CONTINUOUS
At the safe, Arno makes an enormous effort to pry open the door. It begins to give, little by little, and then one last great heave and it swings open.

Janine has moved the drum outside the office, and now she helps Arno put the gold bars in the burlap sacks. When needed they go into the drum to breathe. These are not gold bricks but smaller gold bars, which, although dead weight, can be dealt with much more easily.

ANOTHER ANGLE

as Arno takes the bars from the shelves and puts them in the sacks.

Arno and Janine are ready to move. Janine precedes Arno with the drum, careful not to foul the lines and hoses, as Arno follows, dragging the sacks across the floor.

Arno and Janine reach the outside deck of the wreck. Now comes the tricky part of getting the heavy gold up to the surface. Arno ties the two sacks to the drum. Then he gives two sharp tugs on the rope.

160 EXT: JEAN-PIERRE'S BOAT—CONTINUOUS

COQUINA   The rope! Stop it!

Jean-Pierre is trying to control the rope.

161 EXT: UNDERWATER—CONTINUOUS

The jerk of the rope that is attached to the gold bags causes one of them to break loose. Arno gets to it in time and now holds it on top of the ascending drum. Janine is in the drum below him, her legs protruding from the bottom.

The shark knife sits on the sea floor, forgotten.

162 EXT: JEAN-PIERRE'S BOAT—CONTINUOUS
Coquina attends the generator. Jean-Pierre is at the rail handling the rope. He begins to pull. It is very heavy, but the rope passes through a pulley winch, which makes it somewhat easier.

163 EXT: UNDERWATER—ASCENDING DRUM
The gold sacks are on top. Janine is inside. Arno stays at the bottom of the drum, ducking his head inside and out to breathe but also keeping an eye on the gold sacks.

164 EXT: JEAN-PIERRE'S BOAT—CONTINUOUS
Jean-Pierre succeeds in getting a hold on the rope.

JEAN-PIERRE   I'm bringing them up. Why don't we meet on the beach at midnight? You bring Arno's haul.

COQUINA   If you bring yours.

Jean-Pierre lets go of the winch.

JEAN-PIERRE   Okay.

He holds her tight and kisses her. She lets him. The sparks from the flares are flying.

165 INT: DRUM—CONTINUOUS

The drum has stopped ascending. Arno and Janine look at each other.

ARNO I'll see what's wrong.

166 EXT: UNDERWATER—DRUM—CONTINUOUS
Arno swims from the drum to the surface.

167 EXT: SURFACE—CONTINUOUS
Arno comes up, sees Jean-Pierre pulling away from Coquina and beginning to work the winch again. Not knowing what to think, Arno dives down to the ascending drum.

168 EXT: UNDERWATER—CONTINUOUS
Arno swims toward the drum. He sees something.

169 INT: DRUM—CONTINUOUS
Janine waits for Arno in the drum, when suddenly it's rammed by the shark!

Janine screams!

170 EXT: UNDERWATER—CONTINUOUS
The drum is tilted, and the gold hangs in its nets.

Janine is disoriented, her legs flailing from beneath the drum. The shark quickly goes for one of her legs, as she drops her lantern to the ocean floor, which falls next to the shark knife.

The underwater light beam turns red.

Bubbles and thrashing about. Shark teeth. Then—blackness.

171 EXT: JEAN PIERRE'S BOAT—MOMENTS LATER
Arno bursts to the surface.

ARNO   Shark!

Jean-Pierre and Coquina help Arno into the boat. The drum has also surfaced.

JEAN-PIERRE   Janine . . . Janine . . . she's in the drum?

ARNO   (*catching his breath*) I don't know . . . she was below. . . .

Arno rushes to the boat's side.

ARNO   (*cont'd*) Oh, my God!

He dives in.

COQUINA   Arno!

172   EXT: UNDERWATER—CONTINUOUS
Arno is frantically searching.

173   EXT: DRUM—CONTINUOUS
Arno finds part of Janine's bathing suit where it was caught on the bottom of the drum as she was torn away.

174   EXT: SURFACE—CONTINUOUS
Arno surfaces with the ripped cloth in his hand. Jean-Pierre reaches down to take it from him. The drum just bobs up and down in the dark water.

JEAN-PIERRE   (*panicking*) Oh, my God! My God! Janine!

Coquina watches, motionless.

It is silent, except for the sound of rippling water in the dark night.

Jean-Pierre looks up.

JEAN-PIERRE (*cont'd*) Janine . . . Janine . . . !

Jean-Pierre is in shock.

Coquina looks at Arno, who is also in shock. Coquina then moves over to Jean-Pierre and comforts him.

Arno just stares at the two of them.

JEAN-PIERRE (*cont'd*) I should never have let her go down for the gold. Oh, my God—the gold!

They start to pull it to the boat.

175 INT: JEAN-PIERRE'S BOAT—CABIN—NIGHT
Silence. Jean-Pierre, Arno, and Coquina sit around a table with the gold stacked in front of them. Bottles of rum and whiskey are on the table. Jean-Pierre has been drinking heavily.

JEAN-PIERRE (*looking at the gold*) She would have liked being a millionaire.

Jean-Pierre looks at Arno, fire in his eyes.

JEAN-PIERRE (*cont'd*) But you made her go down in that drum.

ARNO We're both to blame.

Coquina is taking all this in.

COQUINA   It *was* your idea, Arno.

Arno is shocked.

ARNO   What?

JEAN-PIERRE   You heard her.

Arno looks at Jean-Pierre silently.

ARNO   (*to Coquina*) It's time to go.

Arno rises.

ARNO   (*cont'd*) Coquina?

Coquina remains seated.

ARNO   (*cont'd*) Coming?

COQUINA   I don't know. . . .

ARNO   What?

JEAN-PIERRE   You've tried to take advantage of all of us.

ARNO   I'm the one who risked his life down there.

Coquina points to the pile.

COQUINA   And this is what you have to show for it.

ARNO   Part of this is yours.

She still remains seated.

COQUINA   I only want the necklace . . . as a memento.

Arno, shocked, takes his share.

ARNO   I'll get it.

Arno quickly leaves the boat, and Coquina tries to smile reassuringly at Jean-Pierre.

176   INT: THE CACA—MOMENTS LATER

Arno goes over to a panel of wood next to the boat's wheel and removes it. It is a secret compartment. He reaches inside, pulls out the necklace, puts it in his pocket.

He reaches in again and pulls out an old World War I gun, wrapped in an oily cloth.

He takes the gun and stuffs it in the back of his pants. He puts his jewels and gold into the compartment and closes it.

He climbs into his skiff and heads toward Jean-Pierre's boat.

177   EXT: JEAN-PIERRE'S BOAT—CONTINUOUS
Arno climbs back on board Jean-Pierre's boat and finds that Jean-Pierre is on the bow, readying for departure.

JEAN-PIERRE   (*to Coquina*) Hurry up.

Arno approaches Coquina, aft. It is quiet, and they can only whisper. Jean-Pierre works forward.

Arno holds out the necklace. Coquina takes it.

Coquina smiles. She points to a spot on the ceiling, by the fishing rods.

A broad smile crosses Arno's face.

Coquina holds up Grandmother's bottle of laudanum.

COQUINA   Courtesy of Grandma, he'll have a nice long sleep.

ARNO   And we'll have the whole shebang.

Arno kisses her.

ARNO   (*cont'd*) Lady pirate. You had me going.

JEAN-PIERRE   (offstage) Coquina.

COQUINA   He thinks I'm leaving with him.

Arno nods as Jean-Pierre arrives aft.

178   INT: JEAN-PIERRE'S BOAT—CABIN—MOMENTS LATER
Coquina finishes pouring the last two glasses of champagne and hands one of the glasses to Jean-Pierre.

JEAN-PIERRE   *Salud!*

ARNO   To Janine.

COQUINA   To Janine.

Jean-Pierre watches the other two drink.

JEAN-PIERRE   To Janine. . . .

He drinks his glass of champagne as well. It is silent.

COQUINA   I learned from her.

In the silence, the boat is bumped gently and there are footsteps on the overhead deck. Arno, Jean-Pierre, and Coquina freeze.

The cabin door bangs open. Ortega and Juanito enter. Ortega's left arm is still bandaged and in a sling. Juanito holds a gun in his right hand. He aims it at Arno. Ortega looks around.

ORTEGA   So, we're having a little celebration, are we?

Jean-Pierre is silent.

ORTEGA   (*cont'd*) Looks like gold in here. Look like gold to you, Juanito?

The gold is stacked on the table before Ortega and Juanito. Juanito smiles, showing gold teeth.

ORTEGA   (*cont'd*) Frisk them.

Juanito starts to frisk Jean-Pierre.

JEAN-PIERRE   Thought we were pals, Ortega.

ORTEGA   That was before you tried to doublecross me.

Ortega is helping himself to the champagne bottle.

JEAN-PIERRE   You'll be getting your share.

Juanito is frisking Arno and discovers Arno's gun. Ortega sees it.

ARNO   Not my share.

ORTEGA   We're all pals, aren't we, Arno? Share and share alike?

A knife materializes in Ortega's hand.

ORTEGA   (*cont'd*) You cut me, I cut you.

With that, Ortega plunges the knife into Arno's upper arm, wounding him.

Arno shrieks with pain. Coquina rushes to Arno, and he motions her to stand back. Ortega coolly folds the switchblade and slides it into his sling. Juanito hands him Arno's gun.

JEAN-PIERRE   Ortega! He doesn't know what he's saying. Take it all—take the damn gold.

Juanito starts packing the gold into a satchel that is on the floor beside the table.

ARNO   His share, not mine.

ORTEGA   Hear that, Juanito? You don't take any gold with Arno's name on it. Now where's the other stuff, J.P.?

JEAN-PIERRE   What stuff?

Ortega, holding Arno's gun, now aims it at Jean-Pierre.

ORTEGA   The jewelry. I know you got it.

Jean-Pierre raises his hands above his head, reaches inside his hiding place in the ceiling, and pulls out a bag as Ortega watches greedily. Jean-Pierre takes the jewelry from the bag and puts it on the table.

ORTEGA   (*cont'd*) There's more in there.

JEAN-PIERRE   Yes, there is.

With his hand inside, Jean-Pierre points the bag at Ortega. He fires a gun hidden inside the bag.

Ortega falls to the floor, dropping Arno's gun, which slides into a corner, away from Arno.

Juanito aims at Jean-Pierre.

Jean-Pierre's gun is on Juanito. Everyone is frozen.

Then Jean-Pierre starts to sway slightly.

Arno looks at Coquina, who reveals the small bottle of laudanum still concealed in her hand. Uh-oh.

It's only a matter of time before Jean-Pierre will succumb to the drug and they are all dead.

Sweat is forming on Jean-Pierre's brow.

Arno catches Coquina's gaze once more and looks down at her feet. His gun is lying on the floor, not so far away.

Arno nods.

With that, Coquina quickly kicks the gun over to Arno, as he hits the floor, going for it. Juanito swings around.

Jean-Pierre fires his gun, and Juanito's chest explodes.

Juanito's body falls right in front of Arno, who is now holding his own gun at Juanito's lifeless head. Arno is shaking but focused.

It is silent, except for Arno's breathing. Coquina is in shock.

JEAN-PIERRE *(cont'd)* Hey, Arno . . .

Arno looks up.

JEAN-PIERRE *(cont'd)* Thanks.

ARNO Coquina . . . hand me that towel.

Coquina, wide-eyed, hands him the towel. Arno wraps his upper arm.

Jean-Pierre tries to catch his breath. Arno looks at him. Then he indicates the bodies of Ortega and Juanito.

ARNO *(cont'd)* What about them?

Jean-Pierre is slurring now slightly.

JEAN-PIERRE They will give the sharks indigestion. . . . *(To Arno.)* Are you able to help me?

Arno helps Jean-Pierre with his good arm, and they start to drag the bodies toward the deck.

JEAN-PIERRE *(cont'd)* Let's dump them on their boat. . . . God, I'm tired. . . .

179 EXT: JEAN-PIERRE'S BOAT—LATER
SUPER CLOSE-UP

as a match strikes and catches fire.

Arno and Coquina watch as Ortega's boat motors slowly away in the distance. It is starting to burn.

180 INT: JEAN-PIERRE'S BOAT—CABIN—CONTINUOUS
The bodies are gone. Drinks are on the table. Jean-Pierre is slumped in a chair. Coquina is bandaging Arno's shoulder.

JEAN-PIERRE *(very sleepy)* Arno . . .

ARNO Yes?

JEAN-PIERRE Listen . . . listen . . . Arno . . . About Janine . . . I would have split with her—fifty-fifty. Honestly. Honest—

He puts his head down on the table and falls asleep.

ARNO Just like Grandma.

COQUINA Let's get out of here. Please.

Arno moves Jean-Pierre's loot bag and the gold satchel to the gangway as they prepare to leave.

181 EXT: CACA—NIGHT

Arno is taking his jewelry and gold from its hiding place on the side of the deck. The gold and loot satchels from Jean-Pierre's boat are there. Coquina comes with two glasses of rum as he joins her at the table.

COQUINA (*toasting*) To us.

They toast and drink.

TIGHT SHOT

as he takes Coquina in his arms, kisses her. It is long, passionate, sensual. He caresses her. She is completely in his power.

ARNO I'll drop you off at Pirate Cay.

She starts to pay attention.

COQUINA Mmmm?

He kisses her.

ARNO If anybody asks, just say I took off on my own. I'll hide out a few days with Orthwell. Then I'll come to get you.

He is stroking her.

COQUINA There's an old ruin of a chapel behind our house. I can hide the stuff there.

ARNO No, I think it's better at Orthwell's. Trust me.

He pours more rum.

ARNO (*cont'd*) It's all ours—imagine, all ours.

COQUINA And I am all yours.

ARNO We can go wherever we want. . . .

COQUINA Tell me again about Paris.

ARNO (*dreamily*) We're in a carriage riding through the Bois
de Boulogne when the chestnut trees are in blossom. . . .

They start to make love.

DISSOLVE TO:

182 EXT: SKY—DAY
*Bright sunlight on placid water. It's the most beautiful place on
earth.*

183 EXT: CACA—DAY
CLOSE-UP

*of Arno's face asleep as the muzzle of a pistol is thrust at his
forehead between his eyes. Arno's eyes pop open. He looks up,
terrified.*

A WIDER ANGLE

*shows Jean-Pierre leaning over Arno, holding the pistol to his
head.*

JEAN-PIERRE All right—where is it?

Arno is in a haze.

ARNO   Where's what?

JEAN-PIERRE   You know damn well!

ARNO   Know what?

JEAN-PIERRE   My take! Cough it up.

Arno tries to sit up and look around. They seem to be alone.

ARNO   Coquina?

JEAN-PIERRE   *Where is she?*

Arno looks at the small table next to him and sees that there is an empty bottle of laudanum sitting there.

Arno jumps to his feet and dashes to his hiding place in the stern. He hastily disengages the panel and thrusts his hand inside. Nothing!

Arno runs down to the stern, looks down, and sees that his skiff is gone! Only a rope is dangling from the stern.

Arno is frozen. Silent. Then he starts to smile. For the first time, Arno becomes aware of the sound of a boat engine.

Jean-Pierre grabs Arno.

JEAN-PIERRE   (*cont'd*) Where did she go? Where is she!

ARNO   (*snapping out of it*) East, west . . . take your pick.

JEAN-PIERRE   Let's find her! *Allons!*

Arno starts to smile.

ARNO   Find her? Okay, you point the way. A beautiful lady loaded with diamonds and gold: Miami, Nassau, Havana, San Juan. . . .

JEAN-PIERRE   It's our gold, dammit. That bitch!

CONSTABLE   (*offstage*) Arno! Jean-Pierre!

ARNO   She one-upped us, that's all. And we showed her how. There's a saying where I come from: The last dog with the bone is the one that gets to bury it.

CONSTABLE   (*offstage*) Jean-Pierre! You there?

JEAN-PIERRE   Bullshit! I'll find her if it's the last thing I do.

ARNO   And if you do—then what?

The Constable's boat motors up to the Caca.

CONSTABLE   (*cont'd*) All right, you two, you're under arrest.

ARNO   Pray tell, what for, Constable?

CONSTABLE   Possession of stolen property.

They begin to laugh, the irony striking them as hysterically funny.

CONSTABLE   (*cont'd*) You laughing at me?

ARNO   No, Constable . . . no . . . the laugh's on us.

184 INT: SILVER SLIPPER BAR—DAYS LATER
Arno walks into the bar, which is sparsely populated. Willie is at the piano.

MAMA NIMA   Got something for you, Arno.

She takes a little package from behind the bar. Arno opens the package while Mama Nima lines up a couple of glasses.

In the package is Arno's watch. He gives it a good look. It's completely restored. Like new.

ARNO   What time you got, Mama?

MAMA NIMA   Three-forty-five.

ARNO   (*smiling*) She fixed it.

He puts the watch around his neck.

MAMA NIMA   You be moanin' all over the bar again?

ARNO   You be listening?

MAMA NIMA   (*putting out the salt*) Squeeze the limes, honey.

They start to drink as the camera moves to Willie, who has been playing. He is now singing "Something for Nothing," and his song continues into and through the next scene, ending as the film ends.

DISSOLVE TO:

185 EXT: A BEACH—DAY

Arno is searching through the flotsam, Dorothy perched on his shoulder. He is feeding her bar nuts. He rubs her head.

He comes upon a tangle of seaweed and extracts a waterlogged yachting camp with PRIDE OF CHICAGO *inscribed above the bill.*

He plunks it on his head, continues through the seaweed, and comes up with a scruffed, soaked leather box, which he pries open. He takes out an ornate diamond necklace and holds it up to the light, a sardonic smile spreading across his face. He's thinking it over. He flings the necklace into the water, takes the box, cocks his cap, and continues on his search of the beach.

DISSOLVE TO:

Full-screen map.

WIDEN OUT

from the small stretch of cays to a view of North America as end credits play and Willie winds up his song.